IT'S NOT HOW MUCH YOU MAKE, IT'S HOW MUCH YOU KEEP

HOW TO AVOID IRS PROBLEMS AND KEEP MORE OF YOUR BUSINESS EARNINGS

Ron Foudy, CPA

Important Notice

While every effort has been taken to ensure that the information contained herein is accurate as of the time of publication, tax laws and regulations are constantly changing.

This book is designed to provide accurate and authoritative information in regards to the subject matter covered, but it is sold with the understanding that the publisher is not engaged in rendering legal or accounting services, and no information contained herein should be construed as legal advice.

If legal advice or other expert assistance is required, the services of a competent professional person should be sought. Please contact the author directly at FoudyCPA.com or (260) 432-4565 for professional assistance.

The publisher does not guarantee or warrant that readers who use the information provided in this publication will achieve results similar to those discussed.

CONTENTS

Chapter 1: Starting Your Business Off Right

Let's imagine a hypothetical scenario. A total stranger walks into my office and asks the following:

---

*"I want to start a business manufacturing this widget that I just got a patent on. It's the best widget in the world, and I know that it's going to be a great widget. It's going to sell like hot cakes, but I'm an engineer. I don't know anything about business. I don't know anything about how to get this thing to market. I have no idea how to go about setting up a company. **Where do I start?**"*

What am I, as an accountant, going to tell this person?

My first question would be to find out exactly what the widget is, and why this person thinks it's going to be a best seller. I'll want to know what kind of research and due diligence he's already done. For example:

- Has he researched similar and competitive products?

- How will his widget be priced compared to the market?

- Where are similar widgets already being sold?

Second, I'd ask about whether or not he has a business plan. This needs to lay our what he thinks can happen in the next two or three years. Usually, most businesses go out of business within about three years after they start.

Next, he needs to choose an appropriate business location. If it's manufacturing, he's going to have to find some facilities that he can set up some equipment to manufacture his widget. He may want to take a look at outsourcing manufacturing, either locally or overseas, depending on how hot this thing is really going to be.

Once you choose a business location, you have to make sure that you have your legal structuring taken care of. He has the option of a sole proprietorship, the most basic business type. If he's going to bring some other investors in it could be a partnership, or perhaps a Limited Liability Company or a corporation. Then, if it's a corporation, you have to decide if it's going to be an S Corporation.

Basically, all of them are taxed fairly similarly for income tax purposes, but there are nuances and benefits, especially as the business grows. If you're a corporation, then you can choose to be an S Corporation, which means your profits are taxed to you on your personal return. Or you can be a regular corporation, also called a C Corporation. Then, the corporation pays its own income taxes to the federal and state governments.

If you are a sole proprietorship or a partnership or a Limited Liability Company choosing to act as a partnership, the downside is that any profits you have are going to be subject to the self-employment taxes. Typically, you'll have another 15% minimum income tax on your profits. Plus, you may have 4%, 5%, 6%, 7% state income tax.

Most of my clients are trying to minimize that self-employment tax. We typically do that with the S Corporation election. For example, let's say they have a $100,000 profit for the year. We may pay out a $50,000 salary, which you do have to pay the 15% payroll tax on. The other $50,000 can still be subject to income tax, but not subject to the payroll tax at 15%. In that scenario you can save roughly $7,500 dollars a year in tax.

The only disadvantage to that process is that it cuts down what your reported Social Security earnings are going to be. Depending on your age, if this guy is, for example, 25 or 30, he may not care that his earnings are not going to be that great for the next few years.

However, for somebody closer to 50 or over, you may be trying to maximizing your Social Security benefits later on in life. Some people try to minimize that all their life, and then they get ready to retire and then they go to Social Security and they find out that because of their low earnings they might only get $600 dollars a month in benefits. If you report higher income during your life, your Social Security benefits are going to be much higher. You must keep in mind your life expectancy in order to avoid short changing yourself.

Next up, you're going to want to register your business with the proper authorities. You want to get a Federal tax ID number. You may or may not have to get a state ID number, depending on what state you're in. If it's a product that you're retailing, you'll probably have to have a sales tax number registration to be able to remit that, unless you're a manufacturer or wholesaler.

Typically, wholesalers will not have to pay sales tax because typically the retail sales tax is paid by the end seller. A wholesaler, in most instances, is exempt from that because they're selling to other businesses. Some companies could wind up being both a retailer and a wholesaler.

Typically, any sales generated within the state your business is located is going to require you to collect sales on in-state purchases. You may also have to collect and remit sales taxes to other jurisdictions, especially if you ship orders out of state. Sales tax compliance can be fairly tricky.

I have had some clients that discover sales tax to be one of the easy things to NOT get set up properly when they start their businesses.

You can quickly build a large unpaid sales tax liability if you don't have things set up properly. When the state finally catches up to you, it won't be pleasant, as most states have strong enforced collections capabilities in regards to sales tax.

Another thing that you're going to need to take into consideration is whether or not you're going to have employees. Along with income tax withholding, you also need to address employment taxes at both the state and federal level, unemployment insurance, worker's compensation insurance, and many other payroll matter. Depending on the size of your payroll, you will have a set schedule for sending money to the IRS. This is usually required monthly, but could be more frequently if you have a large payroll. Addressing IRS tax debts is covered in depth later in this book, but it makes far more sense to never incur these debts in the first place.

The next thing to consider, depending on the nature of your business, is whether or not you need special permits or licenses to operate your type of business. For example, truckers, plumbers, and contractors usually have to have some type of state or city license to operate. If it's a business that you can operate out of your home, for example, then you've got to make sure that you're not running afoul of the zoning regulations in your area.

You're also going to need to create and order various business sundries, such as your business cards, your stationary, etc. You also need to set up your invoicing and accounting systems. A lot of people use QuickBooks or a similar program. Most of these are somewhat easy to work with as long as you have the necessary training to do so, or you might simply choose to outsource this work to your accountant.

Somewhere along this line, you're going to want to consider meeting with an attorney to help make sure you have all your ducks in a row. Either your accountant or attorney can help you set up your legal entity, but you should consult with the other for any other advice on the matter that is more in there realm of expertise. Whether it's a corporation or an LLC, make sure it's being set up properly with the state. Also, you have to think about your insurance. That's an easy one to forget, but you're going to have possibly business property that you want to insure. You may want to have other types of insurance. You want to have liability insurance in case somebody falls on your property, gets hurt and they want to sue you. If you have employees, then you also have to have unemployment insurance that you'll pay to a state, as well as worker's compensation insurance.

Regarding employees, a lot of companies think that when they first need additional hands that they can just start out by treating them as independent contractor and not worry about all this payroll nonsense. Typically, the IRS expects that if you can control how a person does something, where they do it, how they do it, you furnish them tools, that sort of thing, then they're going to consider the person an employee and not an independent contractor.

The IRS routinely conducts audits of independent contractors, and if you get audited for this and the IRS determines you should have treated people as employees, then the penalties and back payroll tax bill can be massive. Also, if you have a retirement plan and you don't treat those people as employees, you could really incur a lot of penalties from the Department of Labor and the IRS for not including those so called independent contractors as employees.

If you choose to handle all payroll matters yourself, understand that there are a myriad of forms that you're going to need to keep track of. You have to fill out the W-4to find out what the exemptions are for the employee. There probably is a correlating state form that you have to fill out. Then you have to have access to the payroll tax withholding schedules. Some people still do manual checks, so you'd have to get the payroll tax table. You could do it through a program like QuickBooks. The trick to doing it yourself is understanding whether or not you're withholding at the correct rate, whether or not you're actually remitting the proper tax. If you wind up not getting the taxes deposited on time, you can easily rack up a 10% penalty real quick on the amount that you are late, even if it's just a week or two. If you have a fairly large payroll you can come up owing not only the tax, but several thousand dollars of penalties and interest.

In all honesty, I typically recommend that payroll is the primary accounting/legal thing you really don't want to do yourself. It's very simple and affordable to have somebody take care of it, an expert, and let them take on the responsibility of doing it all right so you can focus on what you do best.

You could use a company like ADP, for example. The pros of them is that they have their own little program. As long as you have, I'm going to say, simplified systems, not a whole lot of extra withholdings, that you're taking out for the employees, they do a fairly good job. The downside to them is basically you don't have personal contact with anybody. If you have any questions, you have to just call into their call center and wait for somebody to answer the question. If you ever wind up with a penalty, then it's really tough to get ahold of someone that will take care of it for you, and ADP does make mistakes.

Another option to consider is to use a PEO, or employee leasing company. With a PEO, basically all that a company has to do is call in their hours and for the employees. From there, the PEO takes care of cutting all the checks, taking care of all the withholdings, sending all the taxes in. Then when we talk about the payroll tax forms, the PEO will take care of that, also, which every quarter you have to have a Form 941 quarterly payroll tax returns sent in. You may also have state forms that have to be sent in every month with the withholdings. There's state unemployment forms that have to be filed every quarter. There are annual W-2 forms that have to be filed.

There are federal unemployment forms that have to be filed every year. There's a lot of book work and paperwork. Usually the startup company really needs to be spending more time on getting his business up and running and not having to do so much with just making sure that all the paperwork is getting filed properly.

The next thing to think about is how you're going to finance the business. Most people are going to want to have at least 6 months of personal living expenses in savings before starting their own business. The second route to financing is a bank loan. That could be a term loan for equipment or they might give you a bank line of credit. The third way is finding some individuals, friends, that will either loan you money personally or actually invest in the company. The only thing you have to worry about there is making sure you don't run afoul of any securities rules that might be in the state that you're in.

Now let's talk about common small business mistakes. In particular, let's discuss several of the most common issues I see when a small business comes to me that's been around for a while.

Often, the first thing I'm going to do for an established business is look at their books. Some other accountants and tax preparers will just take the client's set of books and not ask a whole lot of questions. They'll just take the numbers off the QuickBooks file and go with it. A lot of times there are adjusting entries that need to be made for one thing or another. Depreciation could be set up wrong or it could be that they're not writing off as much in depreciable expenses, but they could. We want to make the books are in order and proper before really doing anything else.

The next big mistake has to do with the payroll issues we've already discussed on the previous couple pages. Getting behind on your payroll taxes is a big deal in particular. They may not be taking advantage of setting up retirement accounts that could be deductible as an expense. They may not be reimbursing their employees properly for expenses.

Another too common situation: Maybe they chose the wrong entity type to operate under and they're going to have some tax savings by changing to a different type of entity.

There are ways to address this situation, however. Probably the most typical would be that they're operating as a regular corporation that's paying its own taxes and maybe they're wanting to take money out of the corporation. Then they're going to have to take it out as dividends, and then the dividends get taxed at the personal level. You wind up with two layers of taxes, the corporate level and the individual. What we try to do there is switch them over to an S Corporation, saving them some payroll tax, and there's only one level of taxation which is basically the individual level.

Any business also needs to have a set of trusted advisors and consultants to help them succeed.

I'm biased, of course, but an accountant is probably one of the most important trusted advisors to have because you're going to be dealing with them at least yearly if not more often. The accountant can advise you whether or not you're making money. A lot of companies just are operating and they don't really look at their profit and loss statements. As long as they have cash in the bank , they think they're OK. Or maybe they are borrowing money, spend it, and they don't recognize that they're going to have to pay that back sometime.

Maybe they don't have enough profit margin. Can they increase that profit margin? If they can't, they have to decide whether or not they can actually stay in business at that level or can they cut back expenses somehow to be able to make it possible.

The next biggest person you need on your team is an attorney you are comfortable with. They can make sure your legal documents are all in order, plus advise you on how to mitigate certain types of risk in your business.

Third, I think all businesses should have solid banking relationships. If you ever need to do some financing, it can be good to have a banker in your back pocket. This person gets to know and understand your business, making credit decisions easier.

Do you need…
- QuickBooks setup or overhaul?
- Payroll processing assistance?
- Help with a tax debt?

Then call my office directly at **(260) 432-4565** to schedule an appointment.

Chapter 2: Choosing The Right Business Structure

In the last chapter, we briefly discussed the tax situation for self-employed individuals. That discussion applies to small businesses that have chosen not to create a legal entity separate from themselves.

The absolute most simple business structure to set up is the sole proprietorship. The terms self-employed and sole proprietor mean the exact same thing – especially from a tax perspective.

On the federal side, you don't need to do anything special to create a sole proprietorship. As far as the IRS is concerned, as long as you pay those self-employment taxes and file the extra forms required with your personal income tax return, you're in business.

Of course, your state, county, and even city may have additional requirements. The most common requirements are to obtain a local business license and to register a trade name (also known as a DBA – "doing business as").

There are a lot of downsides to operating as a sole proprietor. While beyond the scope of this book, this business type has the greatest liability exposure for the owner. This form of operation also incurs the highest personal tax bill, as we discussed in the last chapter.

A better way to operate is to create a business entity that is legally separate and distinct from yourself as an individual. The most common types of legal entities that you may be familiar with include corporations, partnerships, and the new-fangled LLC (limited liability company).

What this is technically doing is we are now separating your business activity from your own personal self. There are several advantages to creating this sort of separation, including a lot of little things you wouldn't normally consider.

Far and away the two biggest reasons for creating the separate entity, however, are the liability protection and the tax planning benefits.

Let's look at the liability factor. If I offer a delivery service business and I happen to get into an accident, the other person may sue the business. If there is no legal separation between myself and the business, then they are going to be suing me personally. If I have an LLC or corporation, however, they may be limited to just suing the company, providing a layer of protection for myself personally.

The level of risk of your business activity is something you should discuss with an asset protection attorney in order to help determine the best type of business entity for you from this perspective.

Let's talk about the tax side of things. It's pretty common these days to hear people talking about LLCs. This is the most common business entity type to hear about on the radio, TV, and online. The reality is that an LLC isn't for everybody, and it may not be the right type of business entity for you.

More often than not, an LLC is really geared, in my opinion, for either small businesses that won't end up doing much in gross sales or rental properties. In my experience, many businesses are much better off being run as corporations, and they are very similar to an LLC in some regards, but the filing and reporting requirements are a little bit different.

Regardless of whether it's an LLC or a corporation we're talking about, the liability protection is very similar, if done properly. It should also be noted that, while overall audit risk is pretty low either way, your audit is actually lower with an LLC or corporation than it is for a sole proprietorship. This is just one more benefit to setting up the proper entity for your business.

The reason for this is because these business entities are going to have greater reporting requirements than a sole proprietorship. For example, you may be required to report a balance sheet – meaning that you are required to report your assets and debts. This is never required in a sole proprietorship situation.

Due to these enhanced reporting requirements, the IRS often just assumes that everything is going to be reported correctly. This is especially true because of the assumption that more complicated businesses are going to use the services of a professional accountant, such as myself.

When you operate a separate entity, as already mentioned, you're going to have some more reporting and filing requirements. For an LLC or corporation, you're going to have a separate tax return filed for that particular business. Then, the business is going to issue a form K-1 to you personally for use in filing your personal income tax return. This K-1 is similar to a W-2 or 1099 in some regards, but contains a lot more information and can be much more complicated.

In addition, depending on how your company is structured, you may also be set up as an employee of your own company, and thus receive a W-2.

If you set up an LLC and you are the only owner, the IRS will actually classify you as a self-employed, sole proprietorship. This is because under federal law, there is no specific tax treatment for LLCs.

If you create your LLC with two or more owners (technically called "members"), then you will be classified by the IRS as a partnership by default.

These default classifications are usually not in your best interest. For example, accepting the default classification of sole proprietorship or partnership for an LLC does not eliminate the self-employment tax issue.

At the same time, we want to avoid the double taxation element of having a corporation. The double taxation problem arises because, for regular corporations, the corporate entity itself is required to pay income tax on any profits. Then, when these profits are passed on to the owners (shareholders) in the form of dividends, you have to pay personal income tax on that money *again*.

In order to avoid this, most small businesses will opt to be treated as a *small corporation*, referred to as a "subchapter S corporation" for the section of the law that creates this special tax classification. An S-corporation is a pass through entity, meaning that all profits are passed through directly to the owners, rather than being taxed at the entity level. This entirely eliminates the double taxation problem.

Choosing to be treated as an S-corporation is completely optional. In order to elect to be treated this way, you must file IRS Form 2553. There are specific requirements that need to be met in order to file this form, and it can only be done at certain times of the year.

In my experience, the S-corp structure is the best for the vast majority of small businesses. The nice thing about the S-corp is that just about any entity type can select this election. For example, a single owner LLC, a two owner LLC, a 5 owner LLC, and a corporation can all choose to be treated as an S-corporation.

There are specific rules that all S-corporations must meet. For example, they are not allowed to have more than 25 owners, members, or shareholders. There are additional rules regarding the fiscal year of the business, foreign investors, and more. Please call my office at (260) 432-4565 to schedule an appointment to discuss your particular situation and see if you are eligible to elect S-corp status.

For many single-member LLCs, choosing S-corp status can easily save you up to $15,000 per year, even after taking into account the slight increase in your administrative costs associated with the increased reporting requirements for the S-corp. This one thing might prove to be the best tax planning strategy you ever use!

There is one particular requirement of this S-corp strategy that, for some reason, tends to scare some people. Any owners of the S-corp that actively participate in the operation of the business are required to draw some form of paycheck from the business.

The reason for this requirement is simple. As an S-corp, you pay no self-employment taxes on profits that are passed through to you. In fact, you don't pay ANY Social Security and Medicare taxes, period, on any of that pass-through profit. This is actually why we use the S-corp – to save on those exact taxes.

Unfortunately, we can't do this for every dime we take from the company. Part of the same section of law that created this beautiful S-corp benefit was also a requirement that it can't be used to avoid paying all Social Security and Medicare taxes – otherwise nobody would pay them!

The actual money that today's retired seniors paid in to this system their entire life is long gone. All Social Security and Medicare benefits for current recipients is actually paid for by the people that are currently working and paying these taxes. Thus, the IRS is very concerned about the payment and collection of these taxes, because it's what keeps the system going for people currently collecting Social Security benefits.

In order to make sure that all small business owners are paying their fair share into the Social Security and Medicare Trust Funds (these monies are often called "trust fund taxes" by the IRS), everybody at the business is required to be paid *reasonable compensation*, including owners and shareholders.

The definition of what constitutes a "reasonable" paycheck for an S-corp small business owner is one of the most frequently and hotly contested issues every year in tax court. Every year, there are many reasonable compensation cases that go in front of the tax courts, and many more end up in audit situations.

We mentioned earlier that S-corps have lower audit rates than sole proprietorships. The one exception to this, however, is S-corps that don't pay reasonable compensation to their owners. If you want to get audited, this is the fastest way to ensure it happens!

When you pay yourself wages or salary from the business, you pay into Social Security and Medicare. The business still gets to deduct it's half of that money on the corporate return.

So how does this save you money? Let's say your business generates $100,000 in bottom line profit. For what you do, let's say that $50,000 is a "reasonable" salary for yourself. In this example, a self-employed person is going to pay 15.3% self-employment tax on the full $100,000 in profit. The S-corp owner, on the other hand, is only going to pay that tax on the $50,000 in salary. The other $50,000 in profit still requires payment of income tax, but you save that 15.3%. In this example, that's a savings of $7,650 in one year!

So how much salary do you have to take in order to be reasonable, and avoid any risks? This will depend on a LOT of factors, but common things to take into consideration include the salary for somebody in your area doing a similar job, the number of hours you actually work, the responsibilities you take on versus other staff members, and more.

Let's go back to why many business owners don't want to pay themselves a salary (aside from not wanting to pay ANY Social Security taxes!). If you don't currently have any other employees, you're going to need to create a payroll system for just yourself, and this can be quite burdensome.

You're not only going to have to start filing five new tax returns each year to the IRS, but you're also going to have state reporting requirements (unless you live in one of the few states without a state income tax). You're also going to have to make frequent (usually monthly) payments to the IRS and state to pay over those employment taxes.

This extra burden of having a proper payroll process is daunting to most people. Fortunately, an entire industry exists in this country that allows you to outsource this service for a very reasonable fee. Finding the right *payroll processor* to handle all aspects of this for you is quick and painless – and then YOU don't have to worry about it!

Hiring a payroll service for just one employee is very affordable, and worth doing to have it done right. This does eat into the tax savings, of course, but you still come out ahead. Paying a few hundred dollars per year for a payroll service is more than worth being able to save THOUSANDS on your tax bill.

> Please call my office directly to discuss how an S-corporation can save you money: **260-432-4565**.

Chapter 3: Keeping The Books

One of the number one things that gets small business owners into trouble is that they lack a proper recordkeeping system.

In this chapter, we're going to take a look at what kinds of records you should be keeping, why you must keep records, and how to best keep those records. We'll also talk about how long you need to keep certain records for tax purposes

Why do I need to keep books?

Everybody that runs a business, from the smallest home office to the largest multi-national corporation, but maintain certain accounting and financial records. With good records, you'll be able to do accomplish many things, such as the following.

Monitor the progress of your business.   You need good records to monitor the progress of your business. Records can show whether your business is improving, which items are selling, or what changes you need to make. Good records can increase the likelihood of business success.

Prepare your financial statements.   You need good records to prepare accurate financial statements. These include income (profit and loss) statements and balance sheets. These statements can help you in dealing with your bank or creditors and help you manage your business.

- An income statement shows the income and expenses of the business for a given period of time.
- A balance sheet shows the assets, liabilities, and your equity in the business on a given date.

Identify source of receipts. You will receive money or property from many sources. Your records can identify the source of your receipts. You need this information to separate business from nonbusiness receipts and taxable from nontaxable income. After all, you don't want to pay tax on things you don't have to!

Keep track of deductible expenses. The vast majority of the expenses that you incur in the course of operating your business are deductible for tax purposes. A good recordkeeping system will help you capture these expenses when they incur, and save you money on taxes in the long run. You may forget expenses when you prepare your tax return unless you record them when they occur.

Prepare your tax returns. You need good records to prepare your tax returns. These records must support the income, expenses, and credits you report. Generally, these are the same records you use to monitor your business and prepare your financial statements.

Support items reported on tax returns. You must keep your business records available at all times for inspection by the IRS and state tax authorities. If the IRS examines any of your tax returns, you may be asked to explain the items reported. A complete set of records will not only speed up the process, but also ensure that you are not denied any tax benefits to which you are fully entitled.

What kinds of records do I need to keep?

Contrary to popular belief, the law does not require any specific recordkeeping system for your business unless you are publicly seeking investors or offering various types of investments. In other words, you can choose any recordkeeping system suited to your business, as long as it allows you to meet tax reporting obligations.

The business you are in affects the type of records you need to keep for federal tax purposes. You should set up your recordkeeping system using an accounting method that clearly shows your income for your tax year. You should consult with a competent professional for assistance in choosing the accounting method that's right for you.

In the event that you operate multiple businesses, each business needs to have a unique and separate set of records. It is particularly important to keep income and expenses assigned to the right business, and even more important to keep personal expenses separate from business expenses.

In addition, a corporation should keep minutes of board of directors' meetings, even if the only board member is yourself.

Your recordkeeping system should include a summary of your business transactions. This summary is ordinarily made in your bookkeeping system. This system should include your total income, as well as expenses that you are deducting. For most small businesses, the business checkbook or bank statement is the main source for entries in the business books. In addition, you must keep supporting documents, explained later.

What about electronic records? More and more businesses these days are choosing to do ALL their recordkeeping electronically. All requirements that apply to hard copy books and records also apply to electronic storage systems that maintain tax records. When you upgrade from physical records to electronic, you must keep the electronic data for just as long as you need to keep paper copies.

The primary requirement for any electronic recordkeeping system is that the system must be able to display information in a human-readable format. In other words, me, you, and the IRS all need to be able to read what's stored and understand it. If requested by a government regulator, such as the IRS, the electronic system must be able to display records in such a way as to validate whatever it is you're trying to support.

As technology brings us more and more options for recordkeeping, some small business become fearful of migrating 100% to these new systems. However, these systems are not only easier to use, but they also tend to actually be far more affordable than keeping years and years of business records in storage. Once converted to electronic format, the original can actually be safely destroyed. If you would like assistance in switching to a modern electronic system, please give my office a call.

What about supporting documents?

In the normal course of conducting business, you're going to generate a lot of supporting documents. The information from these documents needs to be recorded in your recordkeeping system. These documents might include:

- sales slips
- paid bills
- invoices
- receipts
- deposit slips
- canceled checks

It is important to keep these documents because they support the entries in your books and on your tax return. Keep them in an orderly fashion and in a safe place. For instance, organize them by year and type of income or expense. As mentioned earlier, it is perfectly acceptable to keep these documents in an electronic format.

Let's Talk The Talk, So We Can Walk The Walk
In the course of running your business, you're going to encounter many accounting terms that it can be helpful to have a basic understanding of. Being able to speak the common "language" of business will come in handy when speaking with suppliers, vendors, customers, tax authorities, business managers, consultants, and many other professionals that you'll interact with.

Gross receipts. Gross receipts are the income you receive from your business. You should keep supporting documents that show the amounts and sources of your gross receipts. Documents that show gross receipts include the following.

- Cash register tapes.
- Bank deposit slips.
- Receipt books.
- Invoices.
- Credit card charge slips.
- Forms 1099-MISC.

Inventory. Inventory is any item you buy and resell to customers. If you are a manufacturer or producer, this includes the cost of all raw materials or parts purchased for manufacture into finished products. Your supporting documents should show the amount paid and that the amount was for inventory. Documents reporting the cost of inventory include the following.

- Canceled checks.
- Cash register tape receipts.
- Credit card sales slips.
- Invoices.

These records will help you determine the value of your inventory at the end of the year. Valuing inventory is an important process for tax purposes, and should be discussed with your accounting professional.

Expenses. Expenses are the costs you incur (other than the cost of inventory) to carry on your business. Your supporting documents should show the amount paid and that the amount was for a business expense. Documents for expenses include the following.

- Canceled checks.
- Cash register tapes.

- Account statements.
- Credit card sales slips.
- Invoices.
- Petty cash slips for small cash payments.

A petty cash fund allows you to make small payments without having to write checks for small amounts. Each time you make a payment from this fund, you should make out a petty cash slip and attach it to your receipt as proof of payment.

Travel, transportation, entertainment, and gift expenses.   The rules and recordkeeping requirements pertaining to these particular expenses would take up an entire book of their own. It is very important that detailed records regarding the exact business purpose of these expenses be maintained. In particular, the IRS will require detailed written mileage logs to support this particular deduction. Be sure to keep a mileage log in each vehicle you use for business purposes, and be sure to actually use it. Speak with your tax professional for additional assistance with maintaining these records.

Payroll.   This is another major enforcement area for the IRS and the state. Not only do you have to be concerned with wage and hour laws, but you must also pay employment taxes at specific times. The failure to pay these payroll taxes is a very major offense, and could lead to significant personal liability for the unpaid taxes. Due to the complex nature of payroll, it is highly recommended that you work with a professional on this one!

Assets.   Assets are the property, such as machinery and furniture you own and use in your business. You must keep records to verify certain information about your business assets. You need records to figure the annual depreciation and the gain or loss when you sell the assets. Your records should show the following information.

- When and how you acquired the asset.
- Purchase price.
- Cost of any improvements.
- Section 179 deduction taken.
- Deductions taken for depreciation.
- Deductions taken for casualty losses, such as losses resulting from fires or storms.
- How you used the asset.
- When and how you disposed of the asset.
- Selling price.
- Expenses of sale.

The following documents may show this information.

- Purchase and sales invoices.
- Real estate closing statements.
- Canceled checks.

What if I don't have a canceled check?   If you do not have a canceled check, you may be able to prove payment with certain financial account statements prepared by financial institutions. These include account statements prepared for the financial institution by a third party. These account statements must be highly legible. The following table lists acceptable account statements.

IF payment is by...	THEN the statement must show the...
Check	• Check number. • Amount. • Payee's name. • Date the check amount was posted to the account by the financial institution.
Electronic funds transfer	• Amount transferred. • Payee's name. • Date the transfer was posted to the account by the financial institution.
Credit card	• Amount charged. • Payee's name. • Transaction date.

Proof of payment of an amount, by itself, does not establish you are entitled to a tax deduction. For example, the details on a credit card statement alone are not proof of the business purpose for an expense. You should also keep other documents, such as receipts and invoices, to show that you also incurred the cost and that it was a legitimate business expense.

Recording Business Transactions

A good recordkeeping system includes a summary of your business transactions. Business transactions are ordinarily summarized in books called *journals* and *ledgers*. You can buy them at your local stationery or office supply store, or use bookkeeping software instead.

A *journal* is a book where you record each business transaction shown on your supporting documents. You may have to keep separate journals for transactions that occur frequently.

A *ledger* is a book that contains the totals from all of your journals. It is organized into different *accounts*. If you use a bookkeeping software system, it will replicate these exact same items.

Whether you keep journals and ledgers and how you keep them depends on the type of business you are in. For example, a recordkeeping system for a small business might include the following items.

- Business checkbook.
- Daily summary of cash receipts.
- Monthly summary of cash receipts.
- Check disbursements journal.
- Depreciation worksheet.
- Employee compensation record.

The system you use to record business transactions will be more effective if you follow good recordkeeping practices. For example, record expenses when they occur, and identify the source of recorded receipts. Generally, it is best to record transactions on a daily basis.

Business checkbook. One of the first things you should do when you start a business is open a business checking account at a bank. You should keep your business account separate from your personal checking account in order to avoid confusion and issues with *commingling*.

The business checkbook is your basic source of information for recording your business expenses. You should deposit all daily receipts in your business checking account. You should check your account for errors by reconciling it.

Consider using a checkbook that allows enough space to identify the source of deposits as business income, personal funds, or loans. You should also note on the deposit slip the source of the deposit and keep copies of all slips.

You should make all payments by check to document business expenses. Write checks payable to yourself only when making withdrawals from your business for personal use. Avoid writing checks payable to cash. If you must write a check for cash to pay a business expense, include the receipt for the cash payment in your records. If you cannot get a receipt for a cash payment, you should make an adequate explanation in your records at the time of payment.

Use the business account for business purposes only. Indicate the source of deposits and the type of expense in the checkbook.

Reconciling the checking account. When you receive your bank statement, make sure the statement, your checkbook, and your books agree. The statement balance may not agree with the balance in your checkbook and books if the statement:

- Includes bank charges you did not enter in your books and subtract from your checkbook balance, or
- Does not include deposits made after the statement date or checks that did not clear your account before the statement date.

By reconciling your checking account, you will:

- Verify how much money you have in the account,
- Make sure that your checkbook and books reflect all bank charges and the correct balance in the checking account, and
- Correct any errors in your bank statement, checkbook, and books.

You should reconcile your checking account each month.

Before you reconcile your monthly bank statement, check your own figures. Begin with the balance shown in your checkbook at the end of the previous month. To this balance, add the total cash deposited during the month and subtract the total cash disbursements.

After checking your figures, the result should agree with your checkbook balance at the end of the month. If the result does not agree, you may have made an error in recording a check or deposit. You can find the error by doing the following.

1. Adding the amounts on your check stubs and comparing that total with the total in the "amount of check" column in your check disbursements journal. If the totals do not agree, check the individual amounts to see if an error was made in your check stub record or in the related entry in your check disbursements journal.
2. Adding the deposit amounts in your checkbook. Compare that total with the monthly total in your cash receipt book, if you have one. If the totals do not agree, check the individual amounts to find any errors.

If your checkbook and journal entries still disagree, then refigure the running balance in your checkbook to make sure additions and subtractions are correct.

When your checkbook balance agrees with the balance figured from the journal entries, you may begin reconciling your checkbook with the bank statement. Many banks print a reconciliation worksheet on the back of the statement.

To reconcile your account, follow these steps.

1. Compare the deposits listed on the bank statement with the deposits shown in your checkbook. Note all differences in the dollar amounts.
2. Compare each canceled check, including both check number and dollar amount, with the entry in your checkbook. Note all

differences in the dollar amounts. Mark the check number in the checkbook as having cleared the bank. After accounting for all checks returned by the bank, those not marked in your checkbook are your outstanding checks.
3. Prepare a bank reconciliation.
4. Update your checkbook and journals for items shown on the reconciliation as not recorded (such as service charges) or recorded incorrectly.

At this point, the adjusted bank statement balance should equal your adjusted checkbook balance. If you still have differences, check the previous steps to find the errors.

Types of Bookkeeping Systems

There are two general types of bookkeeping systems that you can choose from: Single-entry and double-entry. You must decide whether to use a single-entry or a double-entry bookkeeping system. The single-entry system of bookkeeping is the simplest to maintain, but it may not be suitable for everyone. You may find the double-entry system better because it has built-in checks and balances to assure accuracy and control.

Single-entry.   A single-entry system is based on the income statement (profit or loss statement). It can be a simple and practical system if you are starting a small business. The system records the flow of income and expenses through the use of:

1. A daily summary of cash receipts, and
2. Monthly summaries of cash receipts and disbursements.

Double-entry.   A double-entry bookkeeping system uses journals and ledgers. Transactions are first entered in a journal and then posted to ledger accounts. These accounts show income, expenses, assets (property a business owns), liabilities (debts of a business), and net worth (excess of assets over liabilities). You close income and expense accounts at the end of each tax year. You keep asset, liability, and net worth accounts open on a permanent basis.

In the double-entry system, each account has a left side for debits and a right side for credits. It is self-balancing because you record every transaction as a debit entry in one account and as a credit entry in another.

Under this system, the total debits must equal the total credits after you post the journal entries to the ledger accounts. If the amounts do not balance, you have made an error and you must find and correct it.

An example of a journal entry exhibiting a payment of rent in October is shown next.

Computerized System

There are computer software packages you can use for recordkeeping. They can be purchased in many retail stores. These packages are very helpful and relatively easy to use; they require very little knowledge of bookkeeping and accounting. The new era of cloud-based bookkeeping systems are even easier to use, and most of them can import transactions directly from your bank and credit card issuers via their online banking systems.

If you use a computerized system, you must be able to produce sufficient legible records to support and verify entries made on your return and determine your correct tax liability. To meet this qualification, the machine-sensible records must reconcile with your books and return. These records must provide enough detail to identify the underlying source documents.

You must also keep all machine-sensible records and a complete description of the computerized portion of your recordkeeping system. This documentation must be sufficiently detailed to show all of the following items.

- Functions being performed as the data flows through the system.
- Controls used to ensure accurate and reliable processing.
- Controls used to prevent the unauthorized addition, alteration, or deletion of retained records.
- Charts of accounts and detailed account descriptions.

How Long To Keep Records

You must keep your records as long as they may be needed for the administration of any provision of the Internal Revenue Code. Generally, this means you must keep records that support an item of income or deduction on a return until the period of limitations for that return runs out.

The period of limitations is the period of time in which you can amend your return to claim a credit or refund, or the IRS can assess additional tax. Table 1 contains the periods of limitations that apply to income tax returns. Unless otherwise stated, the years refer to the period after the return was filed. Returns filed before the due date are treated as filed on the due date.

Keep copies of your filed tax returns. They help in preparing future tax returns and making computations if you file an amended return.

Employment taxes.   If you have employees, you must keep all employment tax records for at least 4 years after the date the tax becomes due or is paid, whichever is later.

Assets.   Keep records relating to property until the period of limitations expires for the year in which you dispose of the property in a taxable disposition. You must keep these records to figure any depreciation, amortization, or depletion deduction, and to figure your basis for computing gain or loss when you sell or otherwise dispose of the property.

Generally, if you received property in a nontaxable exchange, your basis in that property is the same as the basis of the property you gave up, increased by any money you paid. You must keep the records on the old property, as well as on the new property, until the period of limitations expires for the year in which you dispose of the new property in a taxable disposition.

Records for nontax purposes.   When your records are no longer needed for tax purposes, do not discard them until you check to see if you have to keep them longer for other purposes. For example, your insurance company or creditors may require you to keep them longer than the IRS does.

Period of Limitations

IF you...	THEN the period is...
1. Owe additional tax and situations (2), (3), and (4), below, do not apply to you	3 years
2. Do not report income that you should report and it is more than 25% of the gross income shown on the return	6 years
3. File a fraudulent return	Not limited
4. Do not file a return	Not limited
5. File a claim for credit or refund after you filed your return	Later of: 3 years or 2 years after tax was paid
6. File a claim for a loss from worthless securities or a bad debt deduction	7 years

Deducting Business Expenses

You can deduct business expenses on your business or personal income tax return, depending on the form of your business. These are the current operating costs of running your business. To be deductible, a business expense must be both ordinary and necessary. An ordinary expense is one that is common and accepted in your field of business, trade, or profession. A necessary expense is one that is helpful and appropriate for your business, trade, or profession. An expense does not have to be indispensable to be considered necessary.

The following are brief explanations of some expenses that are of interest to people starting a business. There are many other expenses that you may be able to deduct.

Business Start-Up Costs

Business start-up costs are the expenses you incur before you actually begin business operations. Your business start-up costs will depend on the type of business you are starting. They may include costs for advertising, travel, surveys, and training. These costs are generally capital expenses.

You usually recover costs for a particular asset (such as machinery or office equipment) through depreciation (discussed next). You can elect to deduct up to $5,000 of business start-up costs and $5,000 of organizational costs paid or incurred after October 22, 2004. The $5,000 deduction is reduced by the amount your total start-up or organizational costs exceed $50,000. Any remaining cost must be amortized.

Depreciation

If property you acquire to use in your business has a useful life that extends substantially beyond the year it is placed in service, you generally cannot deduct the entire cost as a business expense in the year you acquire it. You must spread the cost over more than one tax year and deduct part of it each year. This method of deducting the cost of business property is called depreciation.

Business property you must depreciate includes the following items.

- Office furniture.
- Buildings.
- Machinery and equipment.

You can choose to deduct a limited amount of the cost of certain depreciable property in the year you place the property in service. This deduction is known as the "section 179 deduction."

Depreciation must be taken in the year it is allowable. Allowable depreciation not taken in a prior year cannot be taken in the current year. If you do not deduct the correct depreciation, you may be able to make a correction by filing Form 1040X, Amended U.S. Individual Income Tax Return, or by changing your accounting method.

Business Use of Your Home

To deduct expenses related to the business use of part of your home, you must meet specific requirements. Even then, your deduction may be limited. You may be able to use the simplified method to figure your expenses for business use of your home.

To qualify to claim expenses for business use of your home, you must meet both the following tests.

1. Your use of the business part of your home must be:
   a. Exclusive,
   b. Regular,
   c. For your trade or business, AND
2. The business part of your home must be one of the following:
   a. Your principal place of business (defined later),
   b. A place where you meet or deal with patients, clients, or customers in the normal course of your trade or business, or
   c. A separate structure (not attached to your home) you use in connection with your trade or business.

Exclusive use.   To qualify under the exclusive use test, you must use a specific area of your home only for your trade or business. The area used for business can be a room or other separately identifiable space. The space does not need to be marked off by a permanent partition.

You do not meet the requirements of the exclusive use test if you use the area in question both for business and for personal purposes.

Exceptions to exclusive use.   You do not have to meet the exclusive use test if either of the following applies.

1. You use part of your home for the storage of inventory or product samples.
2. You use part of your home as a daycare facility.

Principal place of business.   Your home office will qualify as your principal place of business for deducting expenses for its use if you meet the following requirements.

- You use it exclusively and regularly for administrative or management activities of your trade or business.
- You have no other fixed location where you conduct substantial administrative or management activities of your trade or business.

Alternatively, if you use your home exclusively and regularly for your business, but your home office does not qualify as your principal place of business based on the previous rules, you determine your principal place of business based on the following factors.

- The relative importance of the activities performed at each location.
- If the relative importance factor does not determine your principal place of business, the time spent at each location.

If, after considering your business locations, your home cannot be identified as your principal place of business, you cannot deduct home office expenses.

Vehicle Expenses

If you use your car or truck in your business, you can deduct the costs of operating and maintaining it. You generally can deduct either your actual expenses or the standard mileage rate.

Actual expenses.   If you deduct actual expenses, you can deduct the cost of the following items:

- Depreciation
- Registration/Tags
- Parking space/garage rent
- Tolls
- Insurance
- Licenses
- Repairs
- Gas
- Oil

If you use your vehicle for both business and personal purposes, you must divide your expenses between business and personal use. You can divide your expenses based on the miles driven for each purpose.

Standard mileage rate.   Instead of figuring actual expenses, you may be able to use the standard mileage rate to figure the deductible costs of operating your car, van, pickup, or panel truck for business purposes. You can use the standard mileage rate for a vehicle you own or lease. The standard mileage rate is a specified amount of money you can deduct for each business mile you drive. It is announced annually by the IRS. To figure your deduction, multiply your business miles by the standard mileage rate for the year.

Generally, if you use the standard mileage rate, you cannot deduct your actual expenses. However, you may be able to deduct business-related parking fees, tolls, interest on your car loan, and certain state and local taxes.

Choosing the standard mileage rate.   If you want to use the standard mileage rate for a car you own, you must choose to use it in the first year the car is available to your business. In later years, you can choose to use either the standard mileage rate or actual expenses.

Don't be overwhelmed by recordkeeping requirements. For professional assistance in setting up your bookkeeping system, contact us about our "Hassle Free" Setup Service. Call us at **260-432-4565** or visit us online at:

http://FoudyCPA.com

Chapter 4: Taking Care Of Your People

If your desire is to grow a small business beyond what you yourself are capable of handling, you're going to have to hire staff.

With employees comes a whole host of responsibilities: Employment taxes, unemployment insurance, worker's compensation insurance, all sorts of forms and verifications, providing health insurance and other benefits, and more.

Fortunately, there's an easy way to successfully handle these matters without having to handle the compliance burden yourself.

It's called *employee leasing*.

Understanding Professional Employer Organizations

Hiring an employee represents a huge commitment on the part of any company. Whether the position being offered is full-time or part-time, significant investments of time and money are required.

People need to be recruited. People need to be interviewed. Successful candidates need training and benefits. Small businesses and startups can really be hampered by these heavy commitments, and they only become more pronounced as the business grows.

Budgets that are already limited can be thinly stretched, and executive teams can lose valuable time. Many companies are getting around this daunting problem by embracing a simple and innovative solution. Instead of hiring in house, they are beginning to outsource the hiring process to professional employer organizations.

What is A PEO?

A professional employer organization, or PEO, provides services related to human relations, such as payroll, recruiting, employee benefit administration, worker's compensation administration, safety and risk management, and employee training. Outsourcing these tasks allows business owners to focus on their businesses, and make better use of their time and money.

This system goes by several names, including co-employment, employee leasing, or joint employment because even though, for tax purposes, the PEO is the official employer of record, the PEO and the business that is hiring it each have a series of employer responsibilities. The PEO is responsible for paying employees, and handling administration as outlined above. The company is required to manage its employees, and ensure it provides accurate information to the PEO.

A PEO works by leasing out its employees to a client company. Those employees show up to work for the client, but claim the PEO as their legal employer. This creates a system of shared responsibility, where the client no longer has to face the repercussions of crises like sudden changes to compliance requirements or regulations alone. Through the system, small businesses can better weather events that would otherwise prove extremely challenging to profitability.

Who Needs a PEO?
PEOs are generally used by companies with 50 or fewer employees. They serve as a logical choice for small business that cannot afford to hire full-time human relations staff, or simply would prefer not to dedicate time to administrative responsibilities. The National Association of Professional Employer Organizations estimates the average number of employees at a company that uses a PEO to be 19. Still, larger businesses can benefit from a PEO. PEOs can provide them with additional employees to supplement existing human resources assets

Businesses interested in reducing liability often turn to leased employees as well. A business is normally liable to the Internal Revenue Service, as well as other agencies. Equal opportunity cases, and worker's compensation claims can wreak havoc on a company's productive time and budget. A PEO reduces many of these liabilities, allowing small business owners to focus on their core business.

What is the Difference Between a PEO and a Staffing Agency?
There are a few slight similarities between the two, but in general terms, a PEO is vastly different. PEOs have a permanently employed staff, which they deploy to handle the human relations functions at a company. They negotiate health insurance, organize retirement plans, and report wages to the Internal Revenue Service. Staffing agencies provide short-term employees, or staff for specific special projects. They do not administer a company's human resources department. Hiring human relations employees through a staffing agency will not relieve a company's human resources burden.

What is an ASO?
PEOs can be confused with administrative services organizations, or ASOs. The two of them share a similar function, but with one major difference. While ASOs allow for the outsourcing of human resources including benefits administration and worker's compensation, they do not follow the co-employment model. The ASO handles human resources tasks and the filing of tax and insurance documents, but unlike PEOs, the company remains the employer of record. The advantage of this model is that it gives businesses more control over human resources.

Unlike PEOs, they typically don't make an effort to control policies or enact disciplinary strategies. They offer support and advice, but ultimately the company is solely responsible for making any and all final decisions. The one main disadvantage to this system is that it leaves the company without the legal and liability protections that PEOs can provide.

What are some of the Benefits of Using a PEO?
PEOs can provide a host of valuable benefits that reduce hassles and increase productivity. Hiring a PEO means performing fewer administrative tasks. This can lead to more time for employers to put

into their businesses. Another consideration is that business, particularly small businesses, may not have expertise in the intricacies of the laws dealing with payroll benefits and tax reporting. PEOs specialize in this area, and are less likely to make a mistake that might expose a small business to financial or legal harm.

It is also wise to consider the legal protections a PEO can offer. Many PEOs will provide civil defense and employment liability insurance. This can be extremely helpful and cost effective if a former employee decides to sue. Legal matters like wrongful termination and discrimination suits are much less of a burden to companies that use PEOs. Finally, because PEO's are often larger companies, they can negotiate for superior benefits packages at lower rates than a small business could on its own. This makes it possible for small business owners to get a better deal for their employees while maintaining profitability.

Some PEO's offer additional benefits aimed at improving a company's work environment. Quarterly training opportunities can greatly enhance the skills employees can bring to bear for the company. Dispute resolution can save enormous amounts of lost productivity. Portability lets an employer designate a different work site without interrupting the pay schedule.

What are some of the Disadvantages of Using a PEO?
Professional employer organizations can be extremely beneficial to small businesses in particular, but like everything in life, there are a few drawbacks. For instance, small business owners must become used to a loss of control. Small business owners usually involve themselves thoroughly in every aspect of their company. When a PEO takes over, those owners effectively lose control of human resources. Adjusting to the new arrangement can take time.

Health care changes are another very problematic aspect. PEOs are constantly searching for a better, more frugal, health care plan. This means that they are wont to change health care providers on a remarkably regular basis. This has a tendency to be highly frustrating to employees. Companies have the option of addressing by simply using the PEO for strictly administrative purposes, and providing health care services themselves.

What are an Employer's Responsibilities?
Once an employer has formed a business relationship with a PEO, it is prudent to consider what responsibilities the said employer retains. This varies from one organization to another, but generally, the client company must still manage day-to-day operations within the business, establish pay rates, determine policy going forward, and hire and fire employees. Some PEOs will take on the duties of adjusting pay rates, and hiring and firing personnel. This system can release tension between leased employees and those employed by the company.

How Much Does Using a PEO Cost?
Prices can vary from one PEO to another, but as a percentage of a small business' payroll, fees tend to range from about two to ten percent. If an average employee earns $50,000 per year, the company will end up paying around $1,000 to $5,000 per employee per year. Some PEO's charge a simple flat rate, while others are devotees of an a la carte system. Companies are likely to find themselves on the higher end of that spectrum of they have low-wage workers, or require recruitment and training in addition to basic human resources administration. If the company's needs are more basic and its employees earn higher wages, expect to pay prices on the lower end.

No one pricing schedule outshines another. For instance, a per employee, per month rate is vastly superior to a payroll percentage for a company that is growing. However, flat pricing schedules have certain advantages. Flat pricing is the more predicable of the offered price structures. With a flat pricing plan, fees will not go up if employee salaries increase. Comparing companies and prices is highly important because it allows small business owners to understand what makes the most financial sense for their company. Keep in mind that inexpensive programs are not always the most desirable. Programs with attractive price schedules may have achieved those prices by diminishing service.

Companies should be aware that some PEOs will occasionally attempt to hide their fees and downplay the cost of their services. In these cases, the organizations try to focus on the saving they provide through negotiating lower rates for insurance and benefits. Companies need to insist on seeing a full breakdown of all fees and services, in writing, before making the final decision to begin a relationship with a PEO. Transparency is essential to success in business. Finally, consider an organization that allows a company to choose which services it needs, rather than one that provides bundled packages. Companies need the flexibility to pay for only the services they need.

How Do I Choose a PEO?
When selecting from among the 700 PEOs in America alone, there are a myriad of things to keep in mind. For instance, what market does a particular PEO serve? Different states and countries require different certifications for PEOs, so a national or international company needs to know that the PEO being selected can meet its needs. A good choice for a PEO is one with experience and flexible options. Small business owners should also look for one that has previously worked in their industry before making a final decision. There are several other things to consider. Here are a few of the most important:

- **Assess the Company's Needs**
  Decide what benefits and services you need before approaching a PEO. Understanding whether the company needs basic human resources administration, or something more complex, is essential, and allows the PEO to bee of better assistance to you.

- **Seek Referrals**
  Fellow small business owners can be an invaluable resources in choosing the right PEO. They can provide information about a company's responsiveness, pricing structure, and effectiveness. Small business owners should seek out multiple opinions in order to close in on the service that will make their company run more efficiently while reducing costs.

- **Verify a PEOs Accreditation**
  The Employer Services Assurance Corporation is an independent, nonprofit organization. It accredits PEOs, letting small business owners know that they have chosen a company that will be an asset to their business. Accreditation for PEOs can easily be verified within each state.

- **Verify Licensing or Registration**
  Requirements for PEOs vary by state. Making the best selection for a small business involves knowing those regulations. Some states require licensing. Others opt for registration. Still others have no formal regulations. If a state does possess regulations, business owners should seek out a PEO that is compliant.

- **Conduct Thorough Background Checks**
  Professional employer organizations can be a powerful tool to reduce labor, improve benefits, and cut costs. But to take advantage of that, it is necessary to do some further research into the PEO's background. Look into the sixe of the organization, and the number of years it has been in business. Remember to check on its record with the Better Business Bureau.

- **Acquire Pricing and Fee Information in Detail**
  It is absolutely essential to a small business owner's search for the right PEO to ask for a specific breakdown of service fees in writing. This allows for the comparison of prices among services, and ensures a cost-effective business relationship. As mentioned earlier, PEOs can charge fees based on a flat rate, or command a rate that is a percentage of a small business' total payroll. Knowing that data up front can save frustration, as well as time and money.

- **Be a Negotiator**
  Negotiation is essential to securing an organization that does not in any way hinder profitability. The price quoted by a PEO does not need to be final. See if the organization can match or beat a competing price point. Small companies that

are growing quickly have particularly good leverage so press the advantage.

- **Schedule a Meeting**
  A PEOs employees take over a company's human resources department. A small business owner should meet the team that's going to take responsibility for one of the company's most crucial functions. This is a good time to discover whether live customer service is something the organization offers, and if so, the hours during which that service is available. Look into the background requirements for human relations staff, and the medical plans offered by the PEO. Any company needs the maximum amount of information available to make an informed and financially sound business decision.

- **Read Before Signing**
  Once the service contract is signed, the company is committed to it. Before that happens, business owners should be sure of having secured the best deal possible for the company and its employees. Hiring the services of an attorney for this procedure is a lucid step. It should be perfectly clear what services are covered, which are not, and what redress the company may expect if anything unexpected should occur.

  Liability is another thing to consider before signing anything. PEOs are, by and large, honest and reputable services, but some have attempted to get companies to purchase their services by intimating that, due to the fact that the PEO is legally the employer of record, the company retains zero liability. This assertion is patently false. PEOs can reduce, but do not eliminate, liability. They do assume a great deal of the liability an employer would ordinarily bear, including liability for taxes, payroll and benefits, but the employer is still very liable for safety and compliance, Companies should question PEOs concerning liability, and seek legal advice.

The steps detailed above are varied, and labor-intensive, but are necessary for a small business to make the very best use of a powerful tool. Professional employer organizations can administer a company's human resources functions, saving time and money. It can negotiate for better benefits for employees, lower costs, and provide legal protection. Such a uniquely powerful business relationship should be formed with the utmost care.

We are a full-service PEO. To discuss how employee leasing can save you time, money, and frustration, please call my office directly at (260) 432-4565.

Chapter 5: Estimated Taxes

For most small business owners that have not set up a separate business entity, such as an LLC or corporation, one of the first (and biggest) tax surprises that they encounter are self-employment taxes.

When you work a job as an employee, you're probably already aware of the Social Security and Medicare taxes that come out of your paycheck. What you may not be aware of, however, is that the part that you see missing from your paycheck is actually only half of the total IRS bill for Social Security and Medicare taxes.
The other half of this bill is paid directly by your employer. When you're self-employed, you are serving as both employee and employer. In such a situation, congratulations! You get to pay both halves. This is self-employment tax.

Social Security and Medicare taxes combined are going to eat up 15.3% of your self-employment profits. Fortunately, there is a $118,500 cap on the profits you have to pay this tax on (for 2015), but this is of little comfort if your profits are less than this amount.

If you have additional employees in your business, you also need to understand that you're going to be paying one half of their Social Security and Medicare taxes. In this case, they are called "employment taxes". There are also going to be additional taxes you pay for each employee, such as unemployment tax (which pays for unemployment benefits for layed off workers), worker's compensation insurance (in case of workplace injuries). In general, you should budget about 10% of an employee's salary for overhead to pay these additional taxes and insurance.

Now, back to self-employment taxes. You are responsible to take not only the employees portion but you are responsible to pay the full portion to the government on your earnings.

I know that 15.3% seems pretty high. Keep in mind that we are not talking about income taxes here. We are literally only talking about Social Security and Medicare. One of the nice things about being self-employed is you don't have to pay that 15.3% on everything that you earn. Rather, you only pay that on the profit that you end up showing from your business.

Let's take a look at a quick example. Let's say that you have a total of $100,000 worth of revenue for the year in your small business. But, you also have expenses associated with running your business. Let's say that you have $25,000 worth of expenses. That leaves $75,000 in profit.

You will only be required to pay self-employment tax on this $75,000.

Self-employment tax is a shocker to many people. Many small business owners that didn't seek proper advisement from somebody such as myself may find them blindsided by the tax bill associated with this self-employment tax.

But the good news is that with proper planning and budgeting it doesn't have to be such a sticker shock to us. We can actually budget for it, we could work this additional expense into our prices, and plan for it and treat it as an ordinary business expense and continue running our business and continue paying what we need to pay.

When properly budgeted and planned for, you should be paying into your self-employment tax bill four times per year. The IRS requires you to estimate your income for the year. This can be difficult, but there are guidelines for doing this. In general, these estimates are based on your previous year's income. Then, throughout the year you make estimated tax payments to pay both your self-employment taxes AND your estimated income taxes (since there is also nobody else sitting there withholding income taxes from your paycheck!).

Since this estimation process CAN be fairly difficult, especially if your income is seasonal, the IRS allows us to simplify the process and apply a set of "safe harbor" rules. This allows us to generalize our estimated expenses or estimated taxes and not have to pin-point it exactly when we send in the estimated amount. Our goal is to get the amount as close to accurate as possible for when we file the tax return, and this planning process is critical for the self-employed individual. This process is something that we would be happy to assist you with.

The IRS will impose penalties if you fail to make these estimated tax payments, or if the estimates are too low. The 10% underpayment penalty is one more thing that we can help you to avoid.

As we mentioned earlier, if you are an employee, your employer pays half the Social Security and Medicare bill on your behalf. Then, they get to deduct that as a business expense on their business return.

Fortunately, under the current tax rules, you get to do the exact same thing. Even though you still have to pay the full amount of the self-employment tax, you get to deduct one-half of this amount from your taxable income for purposes of calculating your income tax bill.

So that's the federal government. We also have the state to worry about.

The complexity of your state situation will obviously vary depending upon your state of residence. Some states don't have a state income tax, but all states have unemployment insurance that needs to be paid. Here in California, where my accounting firm is based, we have some of the most extensive and complicated state tax reporting requirements in the nation.

The percentages that are charged by all states are going to be less than the federal government, but can still be quite substantial. They need to be treated with the same seriousness as IRS taxes, and should not be ignored. As part of this process, you're going to be paying estimated taxes to the state, also. Most states have aligned their estimated tax payment deadlines with the IRS dates, so that you can just do it at the same time.

Many businesses will forget to take into account the impact of state taxes when creating their budgets (for those that bother to budget!). This is an important conversation to have with your tax professional.

Chapter 6: Tax Debt Options For Tight Times

Sometimes, things get tight. In these situations, there's one creditor that is actually quite easy to get away with not paying on time: **The IRS.**

Unfortunately, once the IRS *does* come knocking, it can get ugly pretty fast.

When you're trying to resolve tax matters with the IRS, you have a number of different options. Depending on your financial circumstances and the amount of your IRS back tax liability and other issues, you have several options available to you. In this chapter we will give you a brief overview of some of these options.

A Brief Word On Offers in Compromise

The Offer in Compromise is probably the most commonly known tax resolution strategy. This is what you hear about in TV commercials and radio ads, particularly when they talk about settling your tax debt for "pennies on the dollar" (a phrase which the IRS has technically banned advertisers from using). However, it is important to keep in mind that not everybody even qualifies for an Offer in Compromise, not to mention that this is only one of the many options that might be available to you.

Each option must be explored in relation to the specific facts and circumstances surrounding your tax problem and then the best option can be selected and implemented. In some instances it may be necessary to employ two or more options to settle your tax obligations. Keep in mind that the ultimate goal is to solve your tax problem permanently and for the lowest amount allowed by law.

Big Option 1 – Full pay the tax owed

While seldom a popular option, sometimes you may have the ability to pay the tax outright or borrow against an existing asset, such as a cash out refinance of the equity in your home. Surprisingly, in this situation this option is usually the least costly of viable options available to you. The reason for this is simple. One, your equity and assets will usually disqualify you from benefiting from options which grant debt forgiveness. Second, until the tax debt is paid in its entirety it will continue to accrue penalties and interest. Generally, the combined penalty and interest rates that the IRS charges you are going to be significantly less than the interest rate you will pay from borrowing the money elsewhere.

Big Option 2 – Filing unfiled tax returns and replacing Substitute for Returns

When resolving a tax problem it is relatively common to have unfiled back tax returns. There are three reasons why it is necessary to file these returns and become current with your filing obligations.

1. Failure to file tax returns may be construed as a criminal act by the IRS and can be punishable by one year in jail for each year not filed. Filing unfiled tax returns brings you "current."

2. Filing unfiled returns to replace Substitute for Returns may lower your tax liability and the associated interest in penalties because the interest and penalties is calculated from the tax debt amount. A "Substitute for Return" (SFR) is when the IRS uses whatever information that they have available to them to prepare a tax return on your behalf. Now, most of the time this tax return that they prepare is not going to take into

account your expenses, your credits, and any allowable deductions. In other words, an SFR prepared by the IRS based just on the copy of your W-2 that an employer filed with the IRS is <u>not</u> going to be in your favor.

3. A settlement cannot be negotiated with the IRS until you become completely current with all filing obligations.

<u>Big Option 3 – Dispute the tax on technical grounds</u>

If there is a technical basis to dispute the amount of tax owed, there are a number of paths to consider, such as filing an amended return if the statute of limitations to file has not expired or filing an Offer in Compromise under Doubt as to Liability criteria. If you are currently in an audit situation and the math on the audit is simply not right then you can contest the tax on these technical grounds by fighting for the correct calculations.

<u>Big Option 4 – Currently Not Collectible Status</u>

If you do not have positive cash flow above the level necessary to pay your minimum living expenses or you lack sufficient equity in assets to liquidate and pay the tax, you may qualify for Currently Not Collectible status (CNC). This is most commonly seen when you are either unemployed or underemployed. In this situation, the IRS places a temporary hold on the collection of the tax owed until your financial situation improves. If over a longer period of time your situation does not improve, you may eventually become a viable Offer in Compromise candidate.

Big Option 5 – Installment Agreements

In the vast majority of cases, the IRS will accept some type of payment arrangement for past due taxes. In order to qualify for a payment plan, you must meet set criteria, which includes the following, among other things:

- You must file all past due returns.

- You must disclose all assets that you own.

- You must provide information regarding your monthly income and monthly expenses.

The difference between your monthly income and allowable expenses is the amount that the IRS will expect to receive from you under the payment plan.

Monthly payments can be expected to continue until the taxes owed are paid in full. However, it is possible to obtain a Partial Payment Installment Agreement (PPIA). A PPIA means that you'll have an Installment Agreement in place until the Statute of Limitations for collection of the tax expires. After the Statute of Limitations expires, the tax literally just goes away, along with all penalties and interest. The date on which the IRS can no longer attempt to collect the tax from you is called the Collection Statute Expiration Date (CSED).

Big Option 6 – The Offer in Compromise

The IRS Offer in Compromise program allows you to pay the IRS less than the full amount of your tax, penalties, and interest, and pay only a small amount as a full and final settlement. This program also has an option for Doubt as to Liability. In these cases you disagree with the amount of the tax assessment and this gives you a chance to file an Offer in Compromise and have your tax assessment itself reconsidered.

The Offer in Compromise program allows taxpayers to get a fresh start. In this process, all back tax liabilities are settled with the amount of the Offer in Compromise. Once the payment amount of the Offer in Compromise is fully paid off, all Federal tax liens are released. An Offer in Compromise filed based on your inability to pay the IRS looks at your current financial position, considers your ability to pay (income minus expenses), as well as your equity in assets.

Based on these factors, an offer amount is determined. You can compromise all types of IRS taxes, penalties, and interest in one fell swoop. Even payroll taxes, which are often the most difficult to resolve, can be compromised. If you qualify for the Offer in Compromise program, you may be able to save thousands and thousands of dollars in tax, penalty, and interest.

Big Option 7 – Penalty Abatements

In most cases penalties make up 10-30% of your total tax obligation. A penalty abatement request can eliminate some or all of the penalties if you have reasonable cause for not paying the tax on time or paying the appropriate amount of tax. Reasonable cause includes the following: prolonged unemployment, business failure, major illness, incorrect accounting advice or bad advice from the IRS. To prevail in a penalty abatement request as in most tax matters, the burden rest with you to be able to adequately document the reasonable cause.

Big Option 8 – Discharging taxes in bankruptcy

Bankruptcy can discharge federal income tax if certain requirements are met. However, this depends upon both the type of bankruptcy and the type of tax owed. Chapter seven is the chapter of bankruptcy law that provides for the liquidation of non-exempt assets and the discharge of dischargeable debts. Chapters 11 and 13 provide for repayments of debt in whole or in part. To discharge taxes in bankruptcy, a number of criteria must be met:

1. Thirty-six months have lapsed from the tax return due date.

2. Twenty-four months have lapsed from the date the tax was assessed.

3. At least 240 days have passed since the tax was assessed and filing of bankruptcy.

4. All of your tax returns have to have been filed.

Big tax resolution option 9 – Innocent Spouse Relief

It is not uncommon to find yourself in trouble with the IRS because of your spouse or ex-spouses' actions. The IRS realizes that these situations do in fact occur. In order to help you with tax problems which are due to the actions of your spouse, the IRS has developed guidelines for you to qualify as an innocent spouse. If the taxpayer can prove that they meet these guidelines then the innocent taxpayer may not have to pay some or all the taxes caused by their spouse or ex-spouse.

Big tax resolution option 10 – Expiration of the Collection Statute

The IRS only has a limited time during which to collect back taxes from you. This time period starts on the date of the assessment of the tax and runs for 10 years. After the 10 years has lapsed, you no longer owe taxes, penalties or interest on that tax period. There are of course exceptions to this rule. You may agree in writing to allow the IRS more time to collect the tax. If you file an Offer in Compromise or if you file bankruptcy, these actions can both cause automatic extensions on the 10-year period. In these situations the amount of time for the IRS to collect the tax is extended usually by the amount of time that the action is in place.

So for example, if you file an Offer in Compromise and it takes six full months for the IRS to process your Offer in Compromise and give you a determination then the statute of limitations on collection is extended by another six months. If the IRS attempts to collect the tax obligation which is expired under the 10-year rule, the taxpayer must inform the IRS in writing that the statute of limitations has expired. Once this notification occurs the tax can be forgiven. So therefore, if you have tax liabilities that the IRS is trying to collect that are more than 10 years old, it is imperative that you calculate the exact Collection Statute Expiration Date or CSED for short and notify the IRS in writing that they are no longer allowed to collect on that tax if the date is passed the CSED.

Chapter 7: Nasty Things The IRS Can Do To You

A Notice of Federal Tax Lien (NFTL) is an encumbrance that establishes a legal claim by the government. It does not result in the physical seizure of your property. A levy, on the other hand, allows the IRS to actually seize wages, cash, or property. Levies are normally divided into two categories. The first category includes tangible, real and personal property that you own. The second category includes third parties who hold property belonging to you such as bank deposits and wages.

The first category is often referred to as a "seizure", while the second category is usually referred to as a "levy" or "garnishment". The IRS must file a lien before they can issue a levy and must place a levy upon your property before they can seize your property. Levy action is the usually the most severe collections action the IRS takes against the majority of people that owe back taxes, and it is this type of action that an IRS employee is referring to when they talk about **"enforced collection."**

Federal Tax Liens

Once the IRS makes a valid assessment against you, the IRS is required to give notice and demand for payment within 60 days by law. If you don't pay the taxes owed, a Federal Tax Lien automatically arises and attaches to property and property rights either own directly by you or acquired after the date of the tax assessment.

Both Federal law and state law are relevant in determining the effect of the Federal Tax Lien against you and your property. Federal laws determine whether the tax lien has validly attached and state law aids in determining to what property the lien attaches. Under your state laws certain property may be exempt from the lien.

In general, a tax lien gives the IRS a claim against everything you own, from your home and car all the way to the rusted bicycle in your backyard. The lien also technically attaches to your wages, money in you bank accounts, your retirement accounts, and even the cash in your wallet.

A Federal Tax Lien also impacts your credit score, since it shows up on your credit report. Therefore, the tax lien can impact your ability to obtain loans, rent an apartment, and can even impact your insurance rates and ability to obtain employment if you are a job seeker.

In most cases, a tax lien will jump ahead of many other liens against your property after a 180 day period, unless a particular piece of property is used as collateral for a loan. For example, a tax lien does not jump ahead in priority position over a car loan or a first, second, or third mortgage against your home. It will, however, usually jump ahead of, say, a mechanic's lien against your home.

You may have circumstances where having the lien released would be of benefit to helping you resolve the tax situation. There are three types of lien releases available to a taxpayer that may help you resolve tax liabilities with the IRS.

Certificate of Discharge

A Certificate of Discharge (COD) is the process of removing a single piece of property from being subject to the tax lien, usually so that the property can be legally transferred. For example, if you are trying to sell your house but the presence of the lien is preventing this from occurring, then you would need to obtain a Certificate of Discharge to release the tax lien against your house.

In the vast majority of cases, the IRS will not release a lien against a particular piece of property unless they are somehow going to benefit from it. They will generally approve a Certificate of Discharge if the lien discharge will facilitate the sale of the property in such a way that the IRS will get some money out of it. In other words, releasing the lien will facilitate collection of the tax.

If the government isn't going to see any money out of releasing a piece of property from the lien, it's possible to still obtain a Certificate of Discharge if there is a valid reason. In particular, if the IRS won't be receiving any money, but getting rid of the property will free up cash flow and put you in a better financial position in regards to your income and expenses so that later on down the road you can start paying on your taxes, then the IRS will likely approve a Certificate of Discharge.

If the property in question has no significant fair market value, the COD may also be granted, but this is much more of a hit-or-miss situation.

Lien Subordination

A lien subordination is the process of moving the tax lien down a notch in the prioritization of claims against a piece of property. For example, if you own a house free and clear, and the tax lien is in first position against the house, you can't obtain a mortgage against the house. No lender in their right mind is going to loan you money against that house unless their lien is going to take first position.

The answer to this problem is the lien subordination. The IRS will usually approve the subordination of their lien against a property if the lien that will be taking first position ahead of the tax lien will result in money going to your tax liability.

In the house example, obtaining a subordination of the tax lien in order to obtain a mortgage against the house will result in cash coming from that mortgage. At closing, that cash will go directly to the IRS, the mortgage will move into first position, and the tax lien gets re-recorded in second position.

Remember, paying interest on a loan is almost always going to be cheaper than paying penalties and interest to the IRS.

There are other conditions where a lien subordination will still be approved, even if the IRS isn't going to obtain direct proceeds from doing so. For example, many trucking companies will finance their accounts receivable through a process called factoring. In factoring, a lender pays the trucking company some percentage of their accounts receivable (usually 75% to 90%) up front, and then the lender takes the responsibility of collecting on that account receivable when it's due, usually 30 to 90 days down the road. This way, the trucking company gets money now so that they can buy fuel and make payroll.

When a tax lien is filed, most factoring lenders stop funding. In that case, the trucking company suddenly loses all it's cash flow. In order to enable the funding to continue, a lien subordination can be obtained that move the tax lien to a position below the factoring lender, thereby protecting the lender's claim on those accounts receivable.

Lien Withdrawal

There are rare occasions when obtaining an outright release of the entire Federal tax lien is actually the best way to progress towards a resolution of your tax liabilities. If a case can be made that the withdrawal of the lien will facilitate payment of the tax liability, or is otherwise in the best interest of both the taxpayer and the government, then the government may be open to this.

Another case where a lien withdrawal can be applied for is when you have entered into an Installment Agreement to pay the back taxes and the agreement did not mandate that a lien be filed, particularly a payment plan where the payments are directly withdrawn from your bank account. In these cases, you can often get the lien released as long as you are current with your payments and other tax obligations.

Certificate of Release of Paid or Unenforceable Lien

The IRS is required to issue a certificate of release of lien no later than 30 days after one of the following events occur:

- The tax liability is paid in full.

- The tax liability is no longer collectible. In other words, the 10-year statute of limitations on collections has expired.

- The IRS accepts the bond of a surety company or payment of all taxes owed is to be made no later than six months before the expiration of the 10-year collection statute.

- The taxpayer delivers a cashier's check to the IRS and receives a Certificate of Release of Tax Lien.

Tax Debt Resource

Navigating the IRS lien processes discussed in this chapter can be complicated. For professional assistance regarding your tax lien, please give me a call at **(260) 432-4565**.

Bank Account Levies

An IRS levy is the actual action taken by the IRS to collect past due taxes. For example, the IRS can issue a bank levy to obtain your cash in savings and checking accounts or the IRS can levy your wages or accounts receivable, if you run a business.

The person, company or institution that is served the levy must comply or face their own IRS problems. For example, when the IRS issues a levy against your bank accounts, your bank must comply.

The bank is required to take the funds out of your account to which the levy attaches on the day they process the levy. They must then hold those funds for 21 days and then after the 21 days, send those funds to the IRS. If they fail to do this, the IRS will come after your bank and penalize them. The additional paperwork that the bank or other company or institution is faced with to comply with the levy usually causes your relationship to suffer with the person or institution being levied.

When a financial institution receives a levy on your bank account, it cannot surrender the money until 21 calendar days after the levy has been served. This 21-day waiting period provides you the opportunity to notify the IRS and correct any errors regarding your accounts.

An extension of this 21-day period may be granted by the Area Director of the IRS if there is a legitimate dispute regarding the amount of tax owed. Anytime during the 21-day waiting period the levy can be released. During these 21 days it is imperative that you exercise your appeals rights. In this case, you will want to file a CAP appeal. CAP stands for Collection Appeals Process. When you file a CAP appeal, the IRS must hear your case within five days.

Levies should be avoided at all costs and are usually the result of poor communication with your Revenue Officer. When the IRS levies a bank account, the levy is only for the particular day the levy is received by the bank. As I mentioned, the bank is required to remove whatever amount of money is available in your account that day up to the maximum amount of the IRS levy and send it to the IRS after that 21 day hold period.

This type of levy does not affect future deposits. So if your bank account gets levied today and all the money is taken out by the bank to be sent to the IRS 21 days later, you can make a deposit tomorrow that is not subject to that IRS levy.

An IRS wage levy is quite different. Wage levies are filed with your employer and remain in effect until the IRS notifies the employer that the wage levy has been released. Most wage levies take so much money from your paycheck that you don't have enough money to live on. In most circumstances, an IRS wage garnishment will take 70% to 80% of your entire paycheck. For most taxpayers, wage garnishments are the worst thing the IRS can do to them, and everything possible should be done to avoid this debilitating attack on your personal finances.

Personal Property Levies

The IRS's levy power is extremely broad and does not require that the IRS take you to court. The IRS can use its authority to gain possession of your property to pay any back taxes owed and all they have to do is file a notice in demand of payment, wait 10 days, then file a 30-day notice of intent to levy. After that 30 days, they can then levy. The effect of a levy is to compel you to turn property over to the IRS. Amounts that the IRS gains from a levy or garnishment are applied to your tax debt as follows:

1. The proceeds are applied to the expenses of the levy in sale.

2. Proceeds from the levy are then applied to the tax specifically relating to the levied property.

3. Proceeds are then applied to the delinquent tax liability that caused the whole situation in the first place.

4. Funds collected by a levy are considered to have been paid involuntarily. Therefore, you cannot specify to the IRS how you want those funds applied, which you are normally able to do if you make voluntary payments. This is yet another reason why levies are best avoided.

As we already mentioned, the IRS is required to notify you of its intent to levy you at least 30 days before the levy. This is done thru a notice called a Letter 1058 and states across the top of the notice, "Final Notice of Intent to Levy". When you are issued a Letter 1058 by the IRS, you have broad appeals right that allows you to appeal the proposed action. However, your appeal must be submitted within the 30 day window. If you've recently receive a final notice of intent to levy, please see the Chapter on Appeals to learn how to file a Collection Due Process appeal.

Seizures

The IRS must issue a notice of seizure to the owner of any real property (e.g. real estate) or the possessor of personal property as soon as practicable after the property is seized. This notice has the same effect as the Notice of Levy and can be delivered in person to the owner or possessor of the property or left at your home or normal place of business. Seizures must always be approved by upper IRS management. The supervisor must review your information, verify that the balance is due and affirm that a lien, levy or seizure is appropriate under the circumstances. Failure to give the proper notice will invalidate the seizure and afford you certain legal rights.

Seizures of your residence or business

The IRS is no longer really in the business of seizing homes and entire businesses. These sorts of seizures have become relatively infrequent, largely in due to the adverse publicity that the IRS has received from conducting these actions. The Taxpayer Bill of Rights prohibits the IRS from seizing real property that is used as a residence by the taxpayer for tax amounts of $5,000 or less, including penalties and interest.

The Taxpayer Bill of Rights also only permits a levy or seizure on a principal residence if a judge approves of the seizure in writing. Following the 1998 Restructuring Amendments to the Internal Revenue Code, the process for seizing your home has become incredibly difficult for the IRS, which is a good thing for you.

Wage Garnishments

The IRS wage garnishment is a very powerful tool used to collect taxes owed by bringing your employer into the situation. A wage garnishment cannot only be an inconvenience and an embarrassment but it can also leave you with no money to pay your regular living expenses. Once a wage garnishment is filed with your employer, the employer is required to collect the vast majority of each of your paychecks and send that money to the IRS.

As mentioned earlier, the wage garnishment will usually take 70% to 80% of your paycheck. In addition, if you receive Social Security, the IRS can take up to 15% of each and every one of your Social Security checks. The wage garnishment stays in effect until either the IRS is paid or the IRS agrees to release the garnishment.

A wage garnishment can be appealed through the Collection Appeals Program, just like a bank account levy. In addition, wage garnishments are a situation where seeking assistance from the Taxpayer Advocate can be extremely helpful.

Fair Debt Collection Practices Act

The IRS is subject to the conditions of the Fair Debt Collection Practices Act just like any other debt collector. This Act includes a number of rules controlling debt collection practices.

For example, you cannot be contacted by a Collections Representative of the IRS outside of the hours of 8AM to 9PM, and it also prohibits harassing or abusive behavior from the IRS to you. The IRS may not communicate with you at an unusual time or place which is known or which should be known to be inconvenient to you. The IRS can also not communicate with you regarding your tax liability at your place of employment if the IRS knows or has reason to know that the your employer prohibits you from receiving such communication.

If the IRS knows that you are represented by someone who is authorized to practice before the IRS, then they can also not contact you. This provision does not apply if your power of attorney representative does not respond to the IRS within a reasonable period of time after being requested to do so. That is why it's important that if you hire professional tax resolution representation that you hire a reputable firm that's going to actually do what you pay them to do.

Chapter 8: Of Time & Taxes

Statutes of limitations in regards to tax matters are important for you to understand because the different statutes of limitations give you different rights and responsibilities in regards to the tax matters involved. There are some statutes of limitations that work for you and there are others that can obviously work against you. It is important for you to understand these statutes of limitations when dealing with the Internal Revenue Service so that you aren't chasing a ghost or trying to make a case that can't be made.

From the government's perspective, the statute of limitations restricts your rights in many ways, such as the restriction on claiming a refund of tax you overpaid or limiting initial actions to obtain refunds.

Now, a statute of limitations may also restrict what the IRS can do against you. The statute of limitations restricts them from collecting a deficiency in tax after a certain amount of time, and also prevents the IRS from asserting either civil or criminal cases.

Either way you look at it, the statute of limitations issue provides a date of finality after which actions may not be taken by either the IRS or by you which is why it is essential for you to understand them.

Let's first look at the three-year rules. First, the IRS must assess a tax within three years after the date that you file a tax return. This three-year period also applies to penalties. Now, when is a tax return considered filed for the purposes of this rule? A return is treated as being filed on time even if it's received by the IRS after the return's due date.

Timely filing is determined by the postmark stamped on the envelope by the U.S. Postal Service or by a private delivery service. That is why whenever you send a tax return or other important items such as an Installment Agreement proposal or an Offer in Compromise application, or an Appeal, I highly recommend that you always send it by certified mail with return receipt requested.

There does not appear to be a "bright line" test to determine whether a tax return lacking a required form is a valid return. Courts will typically apply the "substantial compliance standard" to the facts of each case. This means that there must be adequate information on the return to calculate the tax liability even if a required form was omitted. The document must also indicate that it is, in fact, a tax return. An honest and reasonable attempt must be made to satisfy the tax law and you must execute the return under penalties of perjury, which is what you're doing whenever you sign the bottom of a tax return. Next time you have a tax return in front of you, take a look at what you're actually signing.

A complete tax return that lacks a specific required form such as a schedule or attachment is still sufficient to begin the statute of limitations running for assessment purposes. So for example, if you file your 1040 personal income tax return but you forget to include a Schedule E. Your income from that Schedule E is on the front page of the Form 1040. The IRS can't say that you didn't file a timely return and therefore they have to start the clock ticking on the statute of limitations for the assessment of the tax as soon as they get it.

There are special statute of limitations rules that you need to be aware of as well. When the IRS produces a Substitute for Return – which is prepared by the IRS when you don't file the tax return – this does not start running the statute of limitations for assessment.

In order to start the clock running on the 3-year assessment statute of limitations, you have to file a proper tax return yourself. So, if you have been notified by the IRS that they prepared the return on your behalf, it is generally advisable to file a n actual, original return as soon as possible.

A six-year statute of limitations, instead of three years, applies to returns that omit a substantial amount of income. "Substantial" means an amount of income which exceeds 25% of the gross income reported on the original tax return. The limitations period is extended to the tax payer's entire tax liability for that year, not just the omitted items.

This applies only to innocent or negligent omissions of gross income. The six-year limitations period does not apply to fraudulent omissions of gross income. If you fraudulently omit reporting income on a tax return, the tax may be assessed at any time.

Here's a bonus tip for you: The burden of proof rests with the IRS in proving that the 25% omission from income did in fact occur. The IRS cannot solely rely on the amount of unreported income asserted in the Notice of Deficiency they mail you, which they're required to send you by law

The Internal Revenue Code states that the IRS can assess tax or bring a suit to collect an unassessed tax at any time regardless of any statute of limitations for some specific situations. Here are those situations:

1. You fail to file the tax return.

2. A false or fraudulent return is filed with the intent to evade the tax.

3. The tax payer attempts to defeat or evade the tax.

4. Once the tax payer files a fraudulent return, the tax payer cannot later start the running of the three-year statute of

limitations period by filing an amended return to include the omitted income.

Next, let's talk about statute of limitations on collection of a tax. Once the IRS has assessed the tax within the assessment statute of limitations as discussed above, the IRS then has 10 years in which to collect the tax. There are certain events that can extend the statutory period past the 10-year mark, because they actually "stop the clock". These events include:

- filing bankruptcy

- filing certain appeal requests

- entering into litigation with the IRS

- filing an Offer in Compromise

- filing a request for an Installment Agreement

- requesting a military deferment

- filing an innocent spouse defense

With these actions, the statute of limitations is temporarily suspended while that action is being investigated.

The date of assessment is the date the Assessment Officer signs the Summary Record of Assessment. This information can be verified by obtaining an IRS account transcript called a Record of Account, which you can request from the IRS at any time. If the Summary Record of Assessment was not properly recorded, then the assessment is actually not proper. Some penalties have a different assessment date from that of the original tax. In those cases the penalty has a separate Collection Statute Expiration Date (CSED), which is the date that the 10-year period ends.

The IRS can use administrative or judicial methods to collect delinquent taxes. The IRS generally precedes administratively by levying and seizing assets that you own. If the IRS embarks upon this course of action, the levy must occur within the 10-year statute of limitations period. The IRS can also precede judicially by filing a lawsuit against you within the 10-year limitation period.

During a period of time in which an Installment Agreement request is pending with the IRS, the statute of limitations on collections is suspended for a while. The period is 30 days following a rejection of a proposed Installment Agreement or 30 days following the termination of an Installment Agreement.

The statute of limitations on collections is also suspended during an Offer in Compromise investigation. During the time that the IRS is considering your Offer in Compromise, the statute of limitations clock isn't running. It is also not running for the 30 days following the rejection of an Offer in Compromise.

The situation is similar for bankruptcy. A bankruptcy petition prohibits the IRS from assessing or collecting a claim from you which arose prior to the bankruptcy petition being filed. During this period the assessment limitations period – the three- and six-year period as discussed earlier – is suspended, plus a period of 60 days after the discharge of your bankruptcy. The limitation period for collection is suspended during your bankruptcy petition period and for an additional six months after the bankruptcy is discharged.

There are times where an Appeals Officer is involved in your case. The settlement authority of an Appeals Officer is very broad. However, their primary job is to resolve the tax issue expeditiously and to weigh the costs of potential litigation for the IRS.

The appeals process is one where professional negotiation skills can really come in handy. Since the appeals process relies so much upon negotiation, a high percentage of cases are resolved here. It is not uncommon for those of us that are professional tax resolution representatives to simply resolve our clients' cases in the appeals process rather than relying on a field Revenue Officer to work with us.

The biggest thing that you need to remember is that the first step in the collection process is for the IRS to actually assess the tax. Until this occurs, the IRS cannot act to collect on that tax. An assessment is simply what the IRS claims you owe. The most common forms of assessment are summary assessments and deficiency assessments.

Summary assessment will usually represent the amount reflected on a tax return that you filed, whereas a deficiency assessment can occur due to an adjustment being made to a filed tax return, such as the result of an audit, or when the IRS files a Substitute for Return.

If you have questions or concerns regarding an IRS assessment, the best thing you can do is speak with a federally licensed taxpayer representative. Please feel free to call my office at (260) 432-4565.

Chapter 9: Understanding IRS Collections And The Resolution Process

The U.S. Internal Revenue Service is the single largest collections agency in the world. In 2010, the IRS spent over $12.5 billion and employed just under 95,000 people to collect more than $2.3 trillion in tax revenue. Of these 95,000 personnel, over 20,000 are directly involved in enforced collections action against taxpayers that owe back taxes.

Needless to say, this is a bill collector that can have a serious impact on your life, especially given the collections actions they can take that other bill collectors can't.

It is important to understand that the IRS is a slow moving bureaucracy that is highly resistant to change, and is heavily driven by forms and written procedures. This doesn't bode well when it comes to fixing your tax problem quickly, but it does provide a major benefit to working to resolve your tax problem: Their playbook is public record, and they're required to follow it.

Here in this chapter, I'm going to provide you an overview of the flow of the IRS collections process and the tax resolution process. Both processes have a very logical, linear flow. In the chapters that follow, we will discuss specific aspects of the tax resolution process, so that you can jump to the chapter and section that is specifically applicable to you, based on where you are in the linear flow of IRS collections.

Collections Starts With A Tax Deficiency

The IRS doesn't start collections activity against you simply because you file a tax return with a balance due and don't pay it. In fact, the collections process really doesn't even start when the tax assessment is made.

In all reality, the IRS collections process begins with a letter called the Statutory Notice of Deficiency (SNOD). Within the industry, we also refer to this as the "21 day letter". This letter is kicked out by a computer automatically when your "number comes up".

This can actually be substantially after your tax return was filed. For individuals that file their tax return on time (by April 15th), it's not uncommon to get the SNOD two to four months after the end of tax season. For business that are behind on payroll taxes, I've seen cases where it take an entire year before the IRS kicks out the SNOD. This delay has been one of the primary things reported by the Taxpayer Advocate to Congress as a major problem within the IRS.

The SNOD is referred to as the 21-day letter because it gives you 21 days in which to pay the tax before additional penalties and interest will accrue on the tax liability. Nothing "bad" is going to happen to you during this period.

Notice of Federal Tax Lien Filing (Form 668-Y)

If you fail to pay your tax bill during the 21-day period of the SNOD, don't set up a payment plan, and don't contest the validity of the tax bill, then the next automatic step, again performed by a computer, is the filing of a Notice of Federal Tax Lien (NFTL). Under new rules issued in February 2011, the IRS will only file an actual tax lien against you if your total tax debt exceeds $10,000, including any prior years you may owe for.

As discussed earlier, a tax lien attaches to everything you own, including your wages and all your property. In addition, a tax lien is eventually indicated on your credit report, and can impact you in numerous ways, also discussed in the earlier chapter on tax liens.

Notice of Intent to Levy (Form Letter CP-504)

Approximately 30 to 45 days after the filing of an actual tax lien, a computer will again kick out another notice to you. This notice will be titled "Notice of Intent to Levy" and contain a designation in the upper right or lower right corner labeled "CP-504".

When you receive a CP-504, it is important to know one major thing: It has no teeth. It is a letter required to be sent to you by law, to notify you that, because of the tax lien, the IRS has the authority to take serious collections action against, such as levies. In reality, the letter itself doesn't grant any rights to either you or the IRS, but when you receive it, it's important to mark it on the calendar, because 30 days after the CP-504, you're going to get something much, much more important.

Final Notice of Intent to Levy (Letter 1058)

Exactly 30 days after a CP-504 is issued, you're going to get another form letter from the IRS, labeled "Final Notice of Intent to Levy". In the upper right or lower right corner will be "Letter 1058".

Letter 1058 is important for two reasons:

1. It is the first opportunity you have to file an Appeal.

2. Thirty days after this letter, the IRS can actually levy you.

Here's the bottom line thing to understand about the Letter 1058: If you don't file an Appeal of this notice, the IRS *can* initiate levy action 30 days after they send this notice. In other words, you can safely ignore a lien and a CP-504, but <u>you simply can't ignore a Letter 1058</u>.

Does a Letter 1058 mean that the IRS *will* levy you? No, it doesn't, particularly if they don't have the information necessary to issue a levy. For example, if they don't know where you bank and don't know where you work, they can't very well issue a levy.

However, if you still work at the same job that you had when you filed the tax return, the IRS knows where you work, because they received a copy of your W-2 from your employer. Also, if you have in the past given the IRS your bank account number and bank routing number in order to have a refund direct deposited, then they know where your bank is.

Whenever you receive a Letter 1058, you should file an Appeal. In order to do this, file Form 12153, *Request for Collection Due Process Appeal*. Further information about filing this appeal, called a "CDP" for short, is available in the Appeals chapter, later in this book. Normally, in my practice I will file a CDP appeal about 20 days into the 30 day window for doing so, in order to give my client as much time as possible to get their finances in order.

The Cycle Repeats

The cycle of SNOD → NFTL → CP-504 → Letter 1058 repeats itself any time you incur a new tax liability. For individual taxpayers, that means this cycle could repeat itself once per year. For a business dealing with employment taxes, this cycle could basically never end, since payroll tax returns are filed quarterly, and this cycle takes about 4 months to complete.

Revenue Officer Assignment

Your first time through this cycle, your case will exist within a division of the IRS called the Automated Collection System (ACS). ACS personnel are located at several of the largest IRS service centers, including Ogden, UT, Cincinnati, OH, and Philadelphia, PA. The majority of letters you receive from the IRS will be from one of these service centers.

Unless your collections case has special circumstances associated with it, you will usually stay assigned to ACS even if you accumulate two or three year's worth of tax debt as an individual, or 3 or 4 quarters of payroll tax liability for a business. After reaching this threshold, your case will likely be assigned to a Revenue Officer. Revenue Officers (RO) are field agents that live and work in local community all over the United States. There are currently over 14,000 of these personnel working for the IRS.

An interesting thing about the current economic situation is that there are a growing number of taxpayers falling into trouble with the IRS. Because of this, the waiting line for assignment to an RO is many areas of the country is growing longer and longer. Certain taxpayers are bumped ahead of the line, depending on their circumstances. But for most taxpayers, they are waiting longer and longer, which gives them more and more time to get their finances in order and hopefully be able to work out something once they *do* get assigned to a field agent.

I've mentioned several times that there are certain circumstances that will get you assigned to a Revenue Officer much faster. Some of those circumstances include:

- your total tax debt is particularly large

- you have personal tax debt for 3+ years

- you owe payroll taxes and are not actively making Federal Tax Deposits

When you are assigned to a Revenue Officer, the course of your tax case takes a sudden shift for the worse. This is the point at which it is definitely advisable to bring in professional representation to assist you.

The Tax Resolution Process

Whether your case is still assigned to ACS, or if it's been assigned to a Revenue Officer, there is a fairly standard, step-by-step process by which your tax case gets resolved. Since the IRS has their own procedures that employees have to follow, you can always know what the next action from the IRS Collections division is going to be.

In general, these are the steps that you will need to follow to make progress towards a successful and permanent tax resolution:

1. Contact ACS or your Revenue Officer and negotiate a time period of 30 to 120 days in order to get your affairs in order for resolving your tax situation.

2. File appeals on any items which you are eligible to do so.

3. File all past due tax returns, including replacing SFR's.

4. Complete a Collection Information Statement, including supporting documentation, to determine your current financial condition.

5. Determine the best resolution strategy based on your financial condition.

6. Apply for and negotiate towards the chosen resolution strategy.

7. Go through the Appeals process, if necessary.

8. Apply for a penalty abatement, if necessary.

These are the same big picture steps that I follow myself when working with a client.

Chapter 10: IRS Reduced Settlements

Whenever you hear the phrase "pennies on the dollar" in relation to tax resolution, you are hearing a reference to the Offer in Compromise (OIC) program.

The OIC program is intended to give taxpayer's without the financial means to pay their tax debt to pay whatever they have, and then start over. In many ways, an OIC is akin to a bankruptcy filing on taxes only

An Offer in Compromise application will require complete financial disclosure, along with *complete* supporting documentation. Because the government is going to accept less money for the tax debt than what you owe, they are going to go to great lengths to make sure that you actually qualify. Refer back to the recordkeeping chapter of this book for more information about the types of information the IRS would expect you to produce in these situations.

Eligibility

Your eligibility to settle for less than what you owe is directly related to your offer amount. If your offer amount is equal to or greater than the minimum amount calculated using the IRS formula, then you may be eligible to file an Offer in Compromise.

Like other resolution options, the IRS also requires that you:

- have filed all past due tax returns

- are not currently generating new tax liabilities

- agree to properly file and pay on all tax returns, on time, for the next 5 years

- agree to let the IRS keep any tax refunds you would otherwise be due during the time you are paying on the OIC

Failure to abide by these rules will either result in rejection of your offer, or default of your offer agreement and reinstatement of any tax liabilities that were eliminated.

Payment Options

In addition to a small application fee, you are required to make payments on the Offer in Compromise unless you meet low income qualification guidelines for an exception to this rule.

The first payment option is used when you will pay the entire amount of your settlement offer in 5 monthly payments or less. If you use this option, you may pay the entire offer amount when submitting your application, or include a minimum 20% deposit (non-refundable!) and take up to a maximum of 5 more monthly payments to pay off your offer. Using this payment option provides the benefit of not being required to make regular payments on your Offer while it is being processed. Using this option also generally results in paying the smallest possible Offer amount.

The second payment option requires you to make regular monthly payments on your Offer in Compromise while the IRS is considering it. These payments are non-refundable, and the first payment needs to be included with your offer application. This second payment option allows up to 24 months to pay the full amount of your Offer.

Regardless of the payment option you use, your payments must add up to the total offer amount, and your offer amount must be at least your Reasonable Collection Potential (RCP), discussed next.

Keep in mind that penalties and interest continue to build on your tax liability while you make Offer payments, even though ultimately those penalties and interest go away when the Offer is paid off and settled. If you default on your OIC, however, those built up penalties and interested are added back on to your balance and you will be liable for them.

Offer Calculation

Many unlicensed tax resolution salespeople, either through ignorance or simply gross incompetence, will tell everybody that they talk to that they qualify for an OIC, and that the Offer amount is some percentage of what they owe.

In addition to this horrifically unethical practice, many tax resolution firms will also only tout their most successful OIC applications, showing you that they did indeed get 1.2 cents on the dollar for one client, and 4 cents on the dollar for another client, all while failing to inform you that:

> a. Most of their OIC applications for clients were outright rejected, and

> b. of those that were accepted, it was usually only for 50 or 75 cents on the dollar.

The Offer amount is the single most important part of a successful OIC application. Calculating the OIC offer amount is extremely formulaic, and requires a complete and accurate Form 433 to be filled out. The IRS goes through an extensive investigation phase to verify information on your Form 433, looking for other assets you own and income you failed to disclose. The IRS looks at various public records sources, and may even pull a credit report to verify what you've told them (this action doesn't require your direct authorization to the IRS under Federal law).

Within the IRS booklet containing the OIC application, there are versions of the Form 433-A and Form 433-B that are modified slightly for OIC purposes. If you use the PDF version of the booklet (search for "IRS Form 656B"), the calculations are actually carried forward for you to the lines that determine your Offer amount.

The entire purpose of these calculations is to arrive at what the IRS calls your "Reasonable Collection Potential", or RCP. The RCP is the sum of the net worth of your assets plus all of your disposable income for the next 1 or 2 years. In other words:

Settlement Amount = (monthly disposable income x 12 or 24 months) + the net realizable equity in the taxpayer's assets)

Disposable income is monthly income minus allowable monthly expenses. It is important to recognize that the IRS will not allow all expenses that you may actually have. Common disallowed expenses are college tuition payments for your children and credit card payments beyond your minimum payment.

The number of months over which disposable income must be calculated into the offer amount is based on the payment plan option you've chosen. If you're paying the Offer on the 5-month plan, then your remaining income is multiplied by 12. If you're paying on the 6 to 24 month plan, then your remaining income is multiplied by 24. Therefore, it at all possible, it obviously behooves you to choose the 5-month payment plan if you can swing it.

"Net realizable equity in assets" is the quick sale value of the asset (often 80% of Fair Market Value (FMV)) minus any liabilities which are secured by the asset (e.g., a loan). As an example, if a taxpayer has a home worth $100,000 and owes $50,000 on the home, the IRS will calculate the net realizable equity in the asset as follows: ($100,000 x .80) - $50,000 = $30,000. The IRS expects, in this example, that the $30,000 will be included in the Offer amount.

Based on this explanation of how RCP is determined, and understanding that RCP is your minimum offer amount, I hope it is apparent as to why the IRS rejects so many OIC applications. In reality, the best OIC candidates are folks that have very little in the way of assets, and no disposable income. The best OIC candidates often tend to be unemployed and broke.

Application Process – What To Expect

When you file an OIC, a Process Examiner will look over your paperwork to make sure that the Offer application meets all the administrative requirements to be eligible, including properly filled out forms, a complete Form 433, and no unfiled tax returns.

Then, an Offer Examiner will be assigned to actually review the merits and financial aspects of your application. This is the person that verifies assets, orders credit reports, and basically gets very up close and personal regarding every aspect of your financial situation or the financial health of your business.

The Offer Examiner will usually provide you the opportunity to address any inconsistencies they discover in their findings, and to argue on your own behalf for the inclusion or exclusion of certain assets or expenses. More often than not, this is the phase where having a professional representative comes in handy the most, to handle these negotiations for you.

Once the Offer Examiner has all the information they need to either accept or reject your Offer, they will do so, and send you a letter explaining why.

Keep in mind that for Payment Option 2, you must continue to make monthly payments on your OIC while this review process is going on.

If you fail to do so, your offer will automatically be rejected, and the IRS will keep the money you did pay and apply it to your tax liability as they see fit.

Appeals

If your OIC is rejected, you have the right to know why, and also the right to Appeal this decision. More often than not, a dispute over including an asset or expense item will be the argument you take to Appeals. Appeals Officers have the authority to accept or reject an OIC based on their own findings, rather than the findings of the Offer Examiner.

Professional Representation

I've said it before in this book, and I'll say it again: *Certain IRS processes really do necessitate professional representation.*

This is obviously one of them. Whether you need help in calculating your RCP, have been denied a legitimate Offer in Compromise application, or are lost on filing your initial application, let me help. Call my office at (260) 432-4565 for assistance in any of these matters.

Chapter 11: Reducing IRS Penalties With Reasonable Cause Penalty Abatements

There are a lot of common misconceptions surrounding the abatement (removal) of IRS penalties and interest.

First of all, it is important for anybody that owes the IRS money to understand that you will not have interest charges removed. If somebody is trying to sell you on their tax relief services and they tell you that they can have the amount of interest on your tax account reduced or eliminated, they're lying. The provisions within the U.S. tax code for eliminating interest charges on back taxes are extremely limited and extremely specific, and if you owe the money but just simply couldn't or didn't pay it, you DO NOT qualify.

The second thing to understand is that the removal of any penalties is extremely formulaic. You must meet one of the reasonable cause criteria outlined by the Internal Revenue Code. Fortunately, these reasonable cause criteria are much broader and more applicable to more people and businesses than are the criteria for interest abatement. Some of the possible reasonable cause criteria include death or illness in the family, loss of records, and receiving bad advice from a CPA.

It is important to note that the two most common causes for accrual of a tax liability are not considered reasonable cause by the IRS, and most often you will not be able to have penalties reduced for these two reasons. These reasons are:

1. Ignorance of filing or deposit requirements

2. Cash flow problems that leave you without enough money to pay the tax when due

Under special circumstances, the IRS will grant penalty relief due to economic hardship, but it is a hard case to prove and tends to be a longer, more drawn out process through the Appeals division. The granting of this sort of penalty relief can also depend upon which Circuit Court of Appeals district you live in, since different case law has been interpreted in a different court jurisdictions.

Above all, just remember that you can get penalties abated, if you have a good reason that was beyond your control and that can be backed up with proper documentation. And as far as interest charges go – forget about it, the IRS is not going to let you off the hook for those if you actually do owe the tax.

One of the biggest things I am adamant about is correcting the myths, lies, and half-truths perpetuated by unlicensed tax resolution salespeople, and the IRS penalty abatement is one of the things least understood and grossly over-hyped by salespeople in our industry.

The "we can remove interest charges" lie, as mentioned at the start of this chapter, is one of the biggest lies that tax resolution sales people tell their prospects.

There are two, and precisely two, instances in which interest is reduced:

> 1. An IRS employee gives you false information, which you acted on and resulted in the interest. This is one reason why all IRS correspondence should be conducted and followed up in writing.

> 2.Since interest is calculated based on the tax liability, if an amended return is filed and the tax itself is lowered, then the interest is also reduced.

Reasonable Cause Criteria

Now, on to penalties. The IRS charges dozens of different types of penalties, but the three that we most commonly talk about are the late filing penalty, the late payment penalty, and the penalty for not making Federal Tax Deposits. These three penalties combined can add a whopping 65% to your total IRS bill. If your tax debt is more than two years old, you've maxed out all these penalties, and therefore over half your total debt is penalties.

The IRS does actually have a compassionate side, and it's generally found in the penalty abatement process. Penalty abatement applications can also be appealed if initially denied, so you can always get a second set of eyeballs on the issue. The thing to keep in mind is that the IRS has very strict guidelines for granting penalty abatements, and these guidelines are referred to as "reasonable cause criteria".

As mentioned earlier, "we didn't have the money" is NOT a reasonable cause criteria. A drop in revenue, by itself, is insufficient argument for obtaining penalty relief. Any request for penalty abatement simply citing the economic recession will be immediately denied.

Why is this? Here is the IRS' logic: You made the money, and should have paid the taxes at the time on that money. If you are self-employed and receive a check, then you HAD the money, you simply didn't give the IRS their chunk of it. Same goes with payroll taxes for businesses, particularly the trust fund taxes (money you withhold from employee paychecks for income tax and Medicare/Social Security): If you had the expectation to pay some amount of wage, then you theoretically HAD the money sitting somewhere to pay that person, and should have withheld it and turned it over to the IRS. If you couldn't cover the taxes, you shouldn't have had the employee and should have laid people off or cut back their hours.

There are ways to argue around this, and we have done so very successfully, but there has to be some other circumstance. For example, you had the money to pay the tax, but paying the tax instead of something else would have created an "undue hardship".

Examples of "undue hardship" could include a large medical expense that unpaid would have left a condition untreated, or a court ordered payment that, if missed, would have resulted in other legal consequences, or a bill such as a large automobile repair which would have left you unable to get to work and resulted in job loss.

These arguments are difficult to make and require significantly more work than standard reasonable cause criteria applications, but they CAN be won, especially in the Appeals process.

The primary IRS penalty abatement reasonable cause criteria center around natural disasters, loss or destruction of vital business records, bad advice from the IRS or an accounting professional, criminal activity, medical issues, substance abuse problems, and other serious circumstances.

A couple years ago I developed a standard list of questions to ask clients to assist me in preparing their penalty abatement. This list of questions should be given some serious thought before requesting penalty abatement, as you are more likely to get what you want if your request covers one of these areas:

- Were any financial records lost or destroyed?

- Was there any transition in your business that lead to the failure to pay taxes, such as a change of ownership?

- Was there a death or serious illness that directly affected your ability to work or impacted the operation of your business?

- Were you the victim of any embezzlement of funds, theft of valuable property, or identity theft?

- Were there any alcohol or drug abuse issues that affected your business or your personal wage earning capability?

- Was there a natural disaster that impacted you or your business?

- Did you rely on the advice of a CPA or IRS employee in making tax decisions?

- Were there any circumstances that created substantial financial hardship, to the point where either yourself or your business was close to going bankrupt?

These questions cover all of the IRS reasonable cause criteria to one extent or another, so finding an answer to your personal or business situation that covers one or more of these questions is the key to a successful penalty abatement application.

Writing Your Penalty Abatement Request

You can use Form 843, *Claim for Refund and Request for Abatement* to apply for relief from penalties. However, as a tax practitioner, I never have, not even once. The reason is simply because the form only has room for about two sentences in order to explain WHY you are requesting the penalties to be removed. Therefore, you're going to end up writing a lengthy letter anyway that gets attached to the Form 843. Because of this, I simply write a letter for my clients that includes all the same information as the Form 843. My typical penalty abatement letter is 3 to 5 pages long, and some are even longer.

The format of a penalty abatement letter is fairly straightforward. When requesting a penalty abatement, I suggest the following format:

1. Indicate the particular penalty types, tax periods, and penalty amounts that you are requesting to be reduced or removed.

2. Include a very brief introduction about who you are, where you live, your family size, and what you do. For a business, give a very brief description of your business, what it does, and how it does it.

3. Provide the background story to the event that caused the tax bills to go unpaid. Be sure to include very specific details, including names, dates, places, events, etc.

4. After explaining why the taxes weren't paid, explain what actions you took to correct the situation, including an explanation regarding the length of time it took to get the tax situation addressed.

5. For business taxes, explain why other business expenses were paid when the taxes were not.

6. Explain the current state of affairs, including the current status of your personal or business finances, and also the status of meeting your current tax obligations and how you've addressed the back tax liabilities

7. Sign your request under penalties of perjury.

Where To Send Penalty Abatement Requests

If you have or recently had a Revenue Officer assigned to you, send your penalty abatement request to that Revenue Officer.

If you do not have a Revenue Officer: Most of your IRS notices most likely come from one particular IRS service center. Make note of the address of that IRS center, and mail your request their to the attention of "Service Center Penalty Appeals Coordinator".

Penalty Abatement Review Process

Whether it is a Revenue Officer or the service center coordinator that reviews your request, they will make a determination regarding whether they believe your request meets reasonable cause criteria.

If it is determined that your application meets reasonable cause criteria, the person reviewing your request will recommend removal of penalties for certain types and period, based on your circumstances. This recommendation will then be forwarded to a manager for final approval.

If your request is denied, you will be told so in writing. You are entitled to know the exact reason that your request was denied. If you are not supplied with this reason in the initial rejection letter, then you should call or write to that person to request it.

All penalty abatement denials have appeals rights. If your penalty abatement is denied for any reason, be sure that you exercise this right. Call our office at (260) 432-4565 if you need assistance with this appeal process, we'd be more than happy to help you with it.

Chapter 12: Working With IRS Appeals

The Appeals division is one of the IRS' best kept secrets. In my experience, Appeals personnel appear to be under less pressure to collect tax revenue than Revenue Officers, probably due to different criteria for personnel reviews. In addition, Appeals personnel are simply more pleasant to deal with in general, usually lacking the snappy attitude and air of arrogance that is unfortunately common amongst Revenue Officers.

The primary function of Appeals is to offer a "fresh look" at cases. Their functional mandate from on high is, effectively, to prevent cases from going to court, thus saving the government the expense of litigation. Appeals, however, is still an administrative function, and is *not* a court in any way itself.

Appeals works in a very formulaic manner, just like any other IRS division. When you file any sort of IRS appeal, you'll receive a letter notifying you that your case has been assigned to a Settlement Officer (SO). Sometimes, this first letter will include your hearing date, sometimes it won't.

The initial contact from appeals via mail will usually include a request for financial documentation if this information wasn't already in your file when it was passed to Appeals from Collections.

If your Appeal in any way mentions a "resolution alternative", then you will be requested to provide the financial documentation necessary to reach that resolution alternative, such as an Installment Agreement, CNC, or Offer in Compromise.

While it would seem contrary to the fundamental function of the Collections division, well over half of all Installment Agreements I ultimately negotiate for clients are created by a Settlement Officer within the Appeals division. They provide an excellent opportunity to resolve your tax case and prevent it from going back to Collections.

Appeals itself doesn't carry out enforced collections activity such as issuing liens, levies, and seizures, but if they kick your case back to a Revenue Officer, such action is very likely to follow pretty soon.

While there are a number of different actions you can Appeal, here are the primary ones that most taxpayers should take note of:

- Collection Due Process (CDP)

- Collection Appeals Program (CAP)

- Trust Fund Recovery Penalty Assessment Appeals

- Penalty Abatement Denial Appeals

Each of these programs has specific rules, requirements, and procedures. We will take a look at each of them in greater detail from this perspective.

Collection Due Process Appeals

Collection Due Process (CDP) appeals are filed when proposed enforced collection activity is unwarranted because you believe there is a better alternative for resolving the tax situation. In other words, a CDP is what you file when you disagree with proposed levy action. When you receive a Letter 1058, Final Notice of Intent to Levy, a CDP appeal is your response to that notice.

Technically, a CDP appeal can be filed under any of the following circumstances:

- a Notice of Federal Tax Lien is filed against you

- a Final Notice of Intent to levy is received

- a Notice of Jeopardy Levy is received

- your state tax refund is taken by the IRS

You have a window of 30 days from when one of the actions above is taken against you in order to file a CDP. You file a CDP using IRS Form 12153, and it is filed with the Revenue Officer, service center, or other division from which you received the notice.

If you request a CDP hearing on time, it will usually stop the proposed levy action. Because the Appeals division is fairly overwhelmed these days, and CDP appeals have a lower priority than many other appeals types, it could actually be several months before your case is assigned to a Settlement Officer and you obtain a hearing. In other words, filing a CDP appeal is a great way to "buy time" to get your financial affairs in order for obtaining a payment plan.

It should be noted that when you file a CDP request, the statute of limitation that the IRS has for collecting the tax (CSED) is extended day for day while you're awaiting a hearing. Therefore, filing a CDP on a tax that is about to expire may not be the best idea.

If you do not file a CDP on time, you can request what is called an "Equivalent Hearing", and Appeals will still hear your case. However, you do not receive the protection from levy action while awaiting an Equivalent Hearing, and the CSED is *not* extended (which can sometimes be a good thing).

When working with clients and filing a CDP, I will also indicate a collection alternative on the form, and include further explanation such as this on the "other" line of the form:

> "Taxpayer intends to resolve the outstanding liability through an appropriate Installment Agreement. Since a reasonable collection alternative exists, levy action should not take place."

By using this type of language, I'm explicitly stating a case for Appeals to consider.

When you receive your notice from Appeals stating that they have received your request, be sure to look for the following items in particular on that notice:

- your hearing date and time, if scheduled

- whether you are calling them, or they are calling you

- any requests for financial information (Form 433) and the deadline they set for getting that information

Deadlines and appointments set by Appeals are extremely important to keep. If you miss a deadline or a hearing, you won't get another one. If the hearing date is inconvenient because of your work schedule or some other reason, it's OK to call and request another time, they will usually accommodate such a reasonable request.

The financial information that you provide should correlate with your alternative collection option. For example, if you have requested an Installment Agreement, then your Form 433 and supporting documentation should reflect the monthly payment you believe you can pay. Similarly, if you are requesting CNC status, then your financial information should essentially indicate that you are broke and make insufficient income to pay basic living expenses.

If Appeals agrees to grant you a resolution option, then they will draft the agreement and send it to you to sign. As with all paperwork from the IRS, read it very carefully to be sure you are signing what you think you are signing. If unsure, have it reviewed by a competent tax professional that can advise you about what the agreement contains.

Collection Appeals Program

The Collection Appeals Program (CAP) is an interesting critter within the IRS world. CAP is an incredibly time-sensitive program within the IRS, and forces the agency to break most of the speed limits that inherently exist in a bureaucracy. When the CAP program was created by Congress in 1998, the legislation with intentionally worded to create this urgency of action, in order to give provide solutions to taxpayer's issues in a timely manner.

A CAP hearing is requested by filing IRS Form 9423, and is available for the following actions:

- filing of a Federal Tax Lien

- denial of a lien discharge or subordination,

- an actual levy

- a seizure

- Denial of an Installment Agreement request

- Termination of an active Installment Agreement

Whenever any of these actions takes place, you can file a collection appeal request with the office that issued the action. Many times, this will be directly with your Revenue Officer. The beauty of the CAP program is that the IRS is required to give you a hearing between with a manager of the department that filed the action against you within two business days of you filing the request.

Under the tax code, you are entitled to a stay of enforcement when you file a CAP request. If you have a manager conference first, before filing Form 9423, you have two days in which to file it after the manager hearing in order to receive this protection against further levy action. If you are appealing the denial of an Installment Agreement, you have 30 days in which to file the appeal, and you receive this same protection during that time period. Incidentally, a managerial hearing is not required when filing a CAP on the denial or termination of an Installment Agreement.

If you are appealing a seizure action, you have 10 days in which to file a CAP.

Note that sometimes you may be entitled to both a CDP hearing and a CAP hearing for the same notice. However, the IRS only permits you to file one, not both. If you need the time provided by the CDP, then file that one. If you are looking for speedy resolution, look to the CAP program.

In most cases, Appeals is required to hear your and make a determination within 5 days. CAP appeals are the highest priority item in the Appeals universe. During this 5 day period, levy action is stopped if it hasn't been already due to other legal requirements on the government, as mentiond above. The exception to this rule is if Collections personnel believe that the CAP is being filed in order to delay levy action for no other purpose than to prevent collection. For example, people have filed CAP appeals in the past in order to give them a couple days to move money out of the country, or to drain accounts into cash so that the government can't seize it. The IRS calls this a "jeopardy" case, because they think collection is in jeopardy. In these cases, levy action will likely continue.

If Appeals decides in your favor, then Collections is required to act immediately upon that decision. It also goes the other way, however, and Collection action will resume if Appeals sides with the Collections division, unless the 30 day rule mentioned earlier for Installment Agreement denials and terminations applies.

The CAP program can be a great tool for obtaining immediate relief from overly aggressive collections action by the IRS. The program definitely requires that you have all your "ducks in a row" in order to obtain a favorable outcome.

Trust Fund Recovery Penalty Assessment Appeals

The Trust Fund Recovery Penalty (TFRP) is a penalty issued against an individual for failure to pay to the government the income tax, Social Security, and Medicare taxes withheld from employee's paychecks at a business. The TFRP, also referred to as a "6672 penalty" due to the section of the Internal Revenue Code from which it comes, is an administrative (non-court ordered) piercing of the corporate veil.

The IRS will generally attempt to assess the TFRP against anybody it thinks it can. While there are defined procedural requirements for issuing a Letter 1153 that actually proposes the assessment against you personally, it is not uncommon in my experience for a Revenue Officer to skip these procedural requirements and just assume that all business owners or officers should be assessed and send the notice.

In order to successfully appeal a TFRP assessment, it is important to understand exactly who, under the tax code, this penalty can actually be assessed against. In order to be imposed with the TFRP, you must be determined to be **both** "willfull" and "responsible" for not having paid the government the trust fund taxes from the business operations.

In other words, in order to be "responsible", you had to have been the person who's job it was to make Federal Tax Deposits (FTD). You can be considered responsible if it was at all a part of your position within the company, even if it was normally physically done by somebody else. If you have never been in any way responsible for or involved with handling payroll and tax matters at your company, then you have a very solid argument against being "responsible".

Similarly, even if you were "responsible" for making tax payments, the IRS must demonstrate that you "willfully" chose not to. Even if making tax deposits is entirely your job at the company, but you do not have signature authority over the bank account to spend the company's money, and somebody else at the company prohibits you from using company money to make the tax deposits, then that other person is "willfull" in not making the payments.

I have seen tax cases where the TFRP fell entirely upon a company employee, such as a bookkeeper, that wasn't even an owner or officer. This was because the bookkeeper had signature authority over the bank accounts to spend the company's money, and was fully responsible for handling payroll and tax matters, but because cash flow was tight for the business, chose to pay rent, utilities, payroll, etc., in order to keep the business operating, instead of paying taxes.

I have also seen cases where the TFRP fell upon nobody at the company, because one person was responsible, and another person willfull. For example, a small business operated by a husband and wife team could be set up such that one spouse does payroll and handles tax returns, but has no signature authority over the bank account. The other spouse has to sign every check, authorize every expenditure, etc., and it can be clearly demonstrated that the other spouse never has and never will have authority to spend money. In this case, one person is responsible, and the other is willful, but neither person is both, so neither of them is assessed the TFRP.

If the IRS is coming after you for the TFRP of a business that you either work for or own, then professional representation is often highly advisable. However, you can appeal the proposal yourself using either a Small Case Request or a Written Protest.

A Small Case Request is used if each and every one of the proposed penalty amounts, on a per tax period (usually quarter) basis, is less than $25,000. A Written Protest is required if any single tax period exceeds $25,000.

A TFRP appeal is handled by your local Appeals office, and is filed with the person proposing the assessment of the TFRP against you, who then forwards your appeal to the Appeals division.

The major difference between a Small Case Request and a Written Protest is that the Written Protest must be signed under penalty of perjury, whereas a Small Case Request does not.

There is no IRS form for filing this particular type of Appeal. Instead, you should write a letter that includes the following information:

1. Your name, address, and Social Security Number.

2. A copy of the Letter 1153 you were sent.

3. A direct statement saying you want an Appeals hearing.

4. A list of the tax periods you are appealing.

5. A statement explaining why you are not responsible, willful, or both. Specifically, explain your duties,

authorities, and responsibilities at the company, and why these make you not responsible or not willful.

6. For a Written Protest, your last paragraph should state:

"Under penalties of perjury, I declare that I have examined the facts presented in this statement and any accompanying information, and, to the best of my knowledge and belief, they are true, correct, and complete."

Like other Appeals types, you'll receive a letter back from Appeals acknowledging your request, and scheduling a hearing and perhaps requesting other supporting documentation to prove your case.

Penalty Abatement Denial Appeals

If a Revenue Officer or Service Center Penalty Appeals Coordinator denies your request for a penalty abatement, that denial comes with Appeals rights.

When filing an appeal of a penalty abatement denial, do the following:

1. Write a letter back to the person that denied your penalty abatement requesting that your request be sent to Appeals for reconsideration.

2. If you have already paid the penalty, include a Form 843, Claim for Refund, for each tax period you are requesting penalty relief for.

3. Include a copy of your original written request for penalty relief, and a copy of the denial letter.

Appeals consideration of penalties has an additional interesting possibility other than full abatement; Appeals has the authority to settle penalties for less than what is owed, without going through the Offer in Compromise process.

Due to the fact that an Appeals denial of penalty relief comes with the right to sue the Federal government, and Appeals is required to consider the possible of the government having to spend money to defend itself in court, Appeals is granted the authority to settle penalties for less than what is owed based on the potential risk of litigation.

In other words, threatening to sue over your penalties may actually be to your benefit.

About The Author

Ron Foudy, CPA is a member of the American Institute of CPAs and the Indiana CPA Society. He has more than 30 years of experience providing tax, accounting, management consulting, and financial planning services to individuals and small businesses in Indiana. Ron is the founder of the Foudy CPA Group, PC, and also operates a full service PEO to address your payroll and employee leasing needs.

To connect directly with Ron, visit FoudyCPA.com or call (260) 432-4565.